Know Your *Market*

How to Do Low-Cost Market Research

David B. Frigstad

OASIS PRESS BOOKS & SOFTWARE

The Oasis Press®/PSI Research
Grants Pass, Oregon

111594

Published by The Oasis Press®/PSI Research
© 1995 by David B. Frigstad

This publication is designed to provide accurate and authoritative information in regard to the subject matter covered. It is sold with the understanding that the publisher is not engaged in rendering legal, accounting, or other professional service. If legal advice or other expert assistance is required, the services of a competent professional person should be sought.

—from a declaration of principles jointly adopted by a committee of the American Bar Association and a committee of publishers.

Editor: Camille Akin
Design: Scott Crawford

Please direct any comments, questions, or suggestions regarding this book to The Oasis Press®/PSI Research:

Editorial Department
300 North Valley Drive
Grants Pass, OR 97526
(503) 479-9464
(800) 228-2275

Library of Congress Cataloging-in-Publication Data
Frigstad, David B.
   Know your market : how to do low-cost market research / by David
B. Frigstad. -- 1st ed.
    p. cm. -- (PSI successful business library)
   Includes index.
   ISBN 1-55571-341-6 (binder) : $39.95. -- ISBN 1-55571-333-5 (trade
paper) : $19.95
   1. Marketing research.   I. Title. II. Series.
HF5415.2.F73 1994   94-21353
  658.8'3—dc20   CIP

Printed in the United States of America

First Edition 10 9 8 7 6 5 4 3 2 1 0

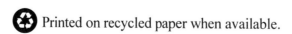 Printed on recycled paper when available.

Table of Contents

Section 1: Market Research Overview

Section 2: The Research Process

Section 3: Tools and Techniques

Section 4: The Role of Reports

Index

Figures

About the Author

David Frigstad, cofounder of Market Intelligence Research Corporation, which became Frost and Sullivan in 1993, has been involved in international marketing challenges for the last fifteen years. These international marketing projects have provided him with a wealth of marketing and sales experience in Europe and Asia.

Mr. Frigstad has developed an in-depth knowledge of industrial and high-technology markets and has extensive knowledge of the unique marketing challenges with which they are faced.

Mr. Frigstad has lectured extensively on market research principles throughout the world and has written several articles relating to high-tech marketing and product development strategies. He also authored several books, including *Market Engineering, Market Research in High Technology, and Customer Engineering.*

Mr. Frigstad holds a Bachelor of Science degree in MIS and received a Master's degree in Japanese Business Administration from the Japan American Institute of Management Science in association with Sophia University, Tokyo, Japan. He also holds a Masters in Business Administration in International Marketing from Indiana University.

Preface

This book is designed to assist small businesses or beginning business owners and executives in conducting their own market research. It is designed to take any individual serious about conducting market research through all the necessary steps to complete a research project. All aspects of the market research function are addressed, including information gathering and utilization and forecasting methodologies. This book will also show you how to acquire and evaluate purchased market research services.

Many market research textbooks are currently available, but our experience reveals that these works can be very complicated and sometimes so divorced from reality that they are virtually useless to today's business executive. Consumer market research has been the focus of extensive attention over the past four decades. Many textbooks analyzing consumer market research exist, and numerous courses focusing on the topic are taught in U.S. business schools.

The exigencies of business in the 1990s and into the twenty-first century allow little time to construct complex models for statistical analysis. Even if the time is available to conduct abstract complicated research, timely and accurate statistics needed to build any type of reliable market analysis seldom are.

Market research is invaluable to any decision making executive. This book works through practical and attainable methodologies we have developed over time. The key words here are practical and attainable. The methods used in this book can be easily employed by you to conduct in-house market research.

Go through the book thoroughly, taking notes. A careful reading of the entire book will help you avoid the host of potential errors that can render a research report worthless — it will save you time in the long run.

Use the worksheets provided in the text, answering questions and addressing issues in a step-by-step manner. This book will save you time by telling exactly what to do from point A to point B, alleviating the majority of concerns generally associated with commencing a research project.

This guidebook is a valuable addition to the libraries of marketing managers, product managers, market researchers, research directors, research and development personnel, strategic planners, vice presidents of marketing, and any executive who must make key decisions as part of their job routing. Any comments, questions, or input you have regarding the content of this book are welcome.

David B. Frigstad
November 1994

Section 1

Market Research

OVERVIEW

Chapter 1

Market Research: Strategic Maneuvering in a Complex Business Environment

Market research is the systematic and organized gathering, analysis, and presentation of information designed to meet management information requirements for strategic and product planning.

Market research involves research into all aspects of a company's market strategy in addition to detailed research on particular markets or market segments.

Market research is not limited to the collection, classification, and storage of data relevant to the marketing function. It also encompasses the design and execution of specific market research studies for management to ensure that its decisions are based upon sound information.

By its very nature, market research must not only be systematic and well organized — it must also be continuous. All factors relevant to the continued smooth functioning of the business operation involving a degree of decision-making by company management should be continuously monitored and evaluated through market research.

The use of market research has both shifted and expanded over the last 20 years. However, the overall penetration of market research as a management tool is far from complete.

In the past, small companies, with sales of less than $10 million per year, did not make significant use of market research. However, now with the use of computers and databases, the usefulness of market research for small companies has increased. Much of the market research that is carried out by smaller companies is comprised of customer information obtained from purchase histories and interests which can be stored and easily retrieved using personal computers. Of the larger companies, only an estimated 20 percent utilize market research significantly, while the remainder undertake moderate or insignificant use.

Typically, market research in markets characterized by high technology growth, rapid change, and innovation is more extensive than in mature markets.

In mature marketplaces, the principal goal is to establish a greater market share by reducing the costs of production, and thus the need for market research is perceived as minimal.

The use of market research is expanding. Changes in the backgrounds of many managers from engineering to financial management are perceived as the primary factor underlying increased use of market research. This new breed of management is generally more likely to appreciate the benefits of market research and encourage its use.

Increases in the availability of purchased market research — either custom or off-the-shelf studies — are also encouraging more widespread use.

To an increasing extent, companies in virtually any market can develop comprehensive databases and libraries of market research information without engaging in significant expenditure on permanent research staff or equipment.

Declining product life cycles and an increased need to continuously innovate and develop new products encourage further use of market research. If a company wants to determine the success of competitor products before introducing competing products of their own, it may be too late.

Product life cycles are shrinking at an accelerating rate, which means that innovation must be continuous — "copycat" strategies will no longer suffice. Timely market research is imperative before funds are allocated to research and development (R&D) to assure the existence of potential markets for new products.

The development of market research has been a rocky road. Despite the resistance to its use since it became prominent following World War II, it appears that the majority of conceptual barriers are being overcome and the real need for this comprehensive and informative business function increasingly recognized.

Role of Research in Marketing

Research plays a big role in any marketing plan. As you develop your research plans, you will need to make critical decisions. In addition, you may need to implement a market information system to regulate the flow of key data. Finally, you must understand the basic difference between market research and marketing research. To get you started, read the following sections.

In essence, management can be defined via its function. Management involves a plethora of tasks that can be broken down to the following:

- Organization
- Staffing
- Direction
- Control

Making decisions is an integral component of all these activities. Managing the marketing function involves making decisions in an attempt to solve problems frequently encountered in marketing.

Because purchasing in consumer product markets is discretionary, research into these markets is important, because it forecasts the percentage of the total potential consumer market that will purchase the product over available alternatives. This research also seeks to determine the comparative timing of those purchases.

Consumer market research revolves around the opinion survey concept. The consumer market is assumed to be homogeneous; samples are determined and questionnaires designed for the appropriate sampling survey.

Research designed to support the marketing function is a tool for marketing management. The research department should be designed to accumulate and analyze information to be used as the basis for recommendations to marketing management on how their problems can best be solved.

A market information system (or MIS) is a formalized system designed to create an organized flow of regular, relevant information for use by marketing decision makers.

The fundamental principle of this concept is that information is collated and analyzed according to a predetermined plan. Methods of reporting accumulated data to decision makers should also follow certain rules.

The structure of the MIS varies widely among firms — both simple and highly complicated systems exist. While computer hardware may be employed as a part of the MIS, it is not absolutely necessary. Larger, more diverse and complicated firms are increasingly using computerized MISs.

MISs providing information on the entire scope of business activity are rare. However, many companies have developed systems focusing on a single component of activity (such as product pricing) with the ultimate goal of integrating separate components into a single comprehensive MIS.

Over the long run, MIS systems are projected to assist in providing heightened acceptance of the apparent advantages of market research. The advantages of having a regular flow of collated and analyzed market data to assist in day-to-day decision making are clear even to those who are skeptical about the perceived benefits of market research. For more information on the role of a MIS for your business, refer to Chapter 9.

The Distinction between Market and Marketing Research

Although market and marketing research are closely related, they differ in both form and intended function.

- Marketing research focuses on the provision of information designed to support tactical decision making in the sales and marketing departments, generally on a short-term basis.

- Market research generally focuses on the long-term and is designed to closely support both strategic marketing and product planning.

The role of market research is to:

- Assist decision makers in establishing goals;

- Provide a standard for company performance in meeting set goals;

- Assist decision makers in solving problems by providing them with timely information;

- Provide information regarding changing end-user demands for product development;

- Assist decision makers in developing optimal pricing strategies;

- Assist management in identifying potential competitive threats;

- Assist decision makers in identifying attractive new markets or acquisition targets; and

- Assist in identifying attractive new technologies.

Critical Marketing Information You Must Have

Behind any successful business is a successful marketing plan. A successful marketing plan does not happen overnight. Instead, it is the result of careful and systematic design. Several critical elements are needed to comprise a comprehensive plan, including:

- A thoroughly segmented market;

- A working knowledge of the market potential;

- A detailed sales analysis; and

- A thorough knowledge of your competition.

Begin with Market Segmentation

The most effective marketing plans are based on a detailed and elaborate understanding of the end-user. Marketing decision makers should have a working knowledge of their purchasing and product preferences, and so on. Often, the majority of a total market can be made up of a few significant end-users, with the remainder of the market divided among numerous smaller end-users. Therefore, the importance of the opinions of certain end-users are far greater than those of others.

Based on this knowledge, marketing decision makers can form a comprehensive profile on the product users. Generally, a number of profiles can be constructed, each describing a different segment of the total market. An attractive market segment must be accessible and suitably large to make market penetration worthwhile. Market research can provide information regarding the segmentation of markets for specific products. In doing so it may identify previously unexploited markets with significant potential. Three primary components of market segmentation exist.

- Geographical segmentation — Markets can be segmented by country, state, or region.

- By type of product — Is the product a component of another product? Is the product intended for a particular end-user?

- By type of end-user — For example, a medical device may be designed explicitly for the home care market, hospital, or outpatient markets.

Accurate and comprehensive estimates of market potential can assist marketing managers in several distinct decision making responsibilities. The capability of the analyst, the research methodology, and the statistical methods used in analysis all have a potential impact on the credibility of the results of market research. Estimates of market potential can help you:

Know Your Market Potential

- Determine sales targets;

- Evaluate company sales performance;

- Formulate appropriate market budgets; and

- Determine appropriate size of sales force.

Estimates of total market potential and market sales forecasts are not the same. The total potential market represents the entire possible marketplace or the sales which would result if market share were completely developed.

Calculate Market Share

Comprehensive market research can provide an estimate of your market share. This data is critical to the development of your marketing function.

Market share is the proportion of total market or industry sales made by one of the competing companies in the market or industry. Market share may be expressed either in commodity unit sales or dollar values, as shown below:

$$\text{Market share} = \frac{\text{Total company sales in commodity units}}{\text{Total industry sales in commodity units}}$$

Alternatively, market share may be expressed as:

$$\text{Market share} = \frac{\text{Total company dollar sales}}{\text{Total industry dollar sales}}$$

Estimating market share by either of these methods involves determining the correct industry and company sales figures for the period in question. The only effective way to acquire this data in a timely manner is through market research.

The value of market share information cannot be overemphasized; this information is the basis for evaluating company performance in the market.

Market share research is never an easy proposition because the majority of firms attempt to conceal their share of the market. In the case of public companies, it is occasionally possible to put together estimates of sales for particular products using 10K annual reports which are filed with the SEC.

Market share estimates can be roughly calculated in interviews with competitors. End-users can also provide valuable market share information. Using an outside consultant to conduct interviews with competitors or end-users can be beneficial because competitors will always be more willing to discuss sensitive information with an independent observer than with a leading competitor.

Like sales information, market share information can be collected to form the basis of forecasting various competitors' shares in the marketplace over a period of time. By comparing the performance of your market share in particular product lines to that of leading competitors, the company can assess the continued profitability of your products. Based on this information, market strategy can be successfully modified to take advantage of any growth in market share, or to make up for any loss of share experienced over time.

Carefully Analyze Sales

Analysis of sales can provide a great deal of detailed market information. A basic sales invoice, itself, contains a wealth of information that is invaluable to the marketing function. The typical information contained in sales invoices are:

- End-user name,
- End-user location,
- Product shipments,
- Shipment dates, and
- Sales territory information.

The importance of this information regarding your company is often overlooked. When this type of data is combined with industry data regarding production costs and product lines, a basis for sales analysis by geographic region, product, and sales region will have been developed. Profit estimates per product line can also be determined.

Sales analysis can be used to effectively evaluate your company's performance in a particular market or market segment. Sales analysis information is crucial in assigning sales territories to sales personnel and in establishing sales quotas for future periods.

In summary, sales analysis is an essential part of any marketing program. The analysis goes far beyond totaling and comparing figures; it can assist in identifying the shortcomings in a marketing program that may otherwise have been overlooked.

Compile Competitor Data

Detailed analysis of competitors is the most efficient way to identify the strengths which distinguish a company from its competition.

To create a detailed market strategy or plan, your business must carry out analyses of the competition. The goal of competitor research is to obtain a perception of the likely strategic decisions a competitor or competitors might make and the potential success or failure of counter-strategies.

A comprehensive competitor analysis should take into account the responses competitors might take to the entire range of potential strategic actions your company might adopt.

A primary objective is to determine your competitors' strategic moves and to estimate the subsequent effects (if any) on your company. Comprehensive competitive analysis can also assess the likely results of your entry into market niches or subsegments.

The real need for competitive information gathering should never be ignored. In practice, competitive analysis is often not carried out at all or is not performed as thoroughly as it should be.

A number of companies have recognized the value of competitive information and have organized systems of competitor intelligence gathering. If these systems are properly organized, they can prove valuable and are generally totally ethical.

Product Development – An Important Stage of Market Research

Market research does not focus solely on research designed to solve marketing problems such as market share estimation, potential market identification, sales analysis, and forecasting.

Once marketing problems have been positively identified by market research, the problems must be solved by action with respect to the product being produced or its price and distribution. The research conducted to assist in making these decisions is product research; the goal of product research is to help solve marketing problems.

Product research is the most difficult and challenging type of market research. Accurate information is crucial when developing a new product because the risk involved in introducing new products is far-reaching.

Leading studies indicate that poorly conducted or insufficiently complete market research is a primary reason underlying the failure of new product introductions. Thus, market research focusing on the introduction of new products is an area that requires considerable care and development.

Develop Your Product Concept

The analysis of a new product concept is a complicated process involving much more than the selection of appropriate market segments. A target market must be selected, the needs of that market assessed, and the product designed with features to suit the needs of that segment.

Many methods are available for developing product concepts. Focus groups are a commonly used technique. After development, product concepts may be assessed using concept-testing methods.

Concept tests determine how readily product concepts are understood, and to what extent the product would meet the needs of the potential users.

Prepare Your Pro Forma Statement

Pro forma statements are planning period forecasts focusing on projected sales, marketing costs, R&D, and other variables. Pro forma statements should be prepared with both pessimistic and optimistic forecasts so that the full range of possibilities can be determined.

Once an appropriate product concept has been determined, a comprehensive business analysis should be carried out, generating one or more pro forma income statements and balance sheets. Management can then determine whether to proceed with product development, based on the pro forma statement projections.

Test Your End-Users

If pro forma statements provide a positive indication regarding the product concept, an end-use testing stage should begin.

End-use testing, involves use of a product by potential end-users under conditions that exist in the target market segment. The end-users provide product evaluations on the basis of the results of beta-site testing.

Use tests are comparatively inexpensive and provide a great deal of product feedback, allowing product improvements to be made prior to the commencement of large-scale production.

Sales Testing. Sales testing can take on several forms, including laboratory test marketing, standard market tests, and controlled market tests. The structure of a test marketing program is generally designed to parallel an actual intended product marketing program, but on a more limited scale.

The test marketing program may involve a variation of the marketing mix so management can determine the ideal blend of marketing variables for the general product introduction.

Test marketing and other forms of sales testing may be conducted for new or existing products when the company is attempting to enter a new market niche or modify an existing product.

The ultimate decision on which type of sales testing to use depends on the type of product information required and the costs the company is willing to incur to acquire the information.

Define Your Product Pricing Strategy

Strategic decisions regarding the ultimate intended price range for the product must be reached early in the product planning stage. To determine the intended price range of the product, it is important to test product concepts, formulate the pro forma statements, and use- and sales-test the product.

Decisions concerning the specific price of the product must be made before product introduction. Two primary pricing strategies are used; the market information required differs depending on the strategy chosen.

The first strategy is designed to enhance market share. The product is introduced at a low price, which is subsequently reduced as sales volume grows and production costs fall. The second pricing strategy introduces the product at a price designed to result in as much profit as possible per unit sold. To set up your pricing strategy you will need:

- Competitor production cost data;

- Data to assist in formulating break-even points;

- Estimates of units sold to each market segment; and

- Product life-cycle projections.

There are three steps to market planning:

- Discovering a way to identify various alternatives;

- Choosing the most appropriate among these alternatives; and

- Pricing and scheduling the steps to achieve objectives.

Market Planning Dynamics

The concept is simple on paper, but it is one of the most difficult marketing functions to organize. All the distinct marketing segments must be brought together into a single, well-developed plan.

Market planning is essential, particularly when considering the increasingly complex business environment in which most companies operate.

Internal and external influences have the potential to impact a firm's ability to achieve its targets for profit maximization, cost minimization, and optimum returns on investment.

The majority of firms have relied on simple sales forecasting and budgeting as their principal sources of information when formulating marketing plans. This data alone does not present marketing management with an accurate picture of the real problems facing their companies.

Information for market planning must include data on competitors, market segmentation, market share, and competing technology, as well as market and company sales forecasts and industry or market growth rates. If up-to-the-minute information on these topics can be given to market managers formulating their plans, the accuracy of these plans will be heightened considerably.

Product Planning Dynamics

Product planning is a vital function in any company. From concept development to product introduction, product development should take place according to a carefully considered, orderly plan.

The function of market research as a product planning tool should be to aid in gathering and organizing new product ideas. Market research can also assist in determining the optimum time for its product development and introduction.

Assisting management in making supported, accurate decisions regarding product development is among the most vital of market research functions. The majority of companies perceive product planning as the primary, if not the only, role of market research.

Companies can often develop a product, then enter a market too early and be disappointed by their sales. Conversely, they may attempt market penetration too late, with the same results. Accurate, timely market research can help minimize these occurrences.

In short, market research can minimize the decision making risks associated with product planning. A real need exists for estimating the potential costs of various alternatives. Market research can effectively help identify which alternatives are best while attaching comparative levels of risk to each one.

Strategic Planning Dynamics

Market research supports the strategic planning function. A strategic plan is a long-term plan, generally stretching up to and over five years. By the very nature of the time period involved in strategic planning, it generally entails major new investment planning.

Short-term operating plans or plans for introducing new products are generally considered tactical, not strategic, plans.

Due to the considerable time periods involved in strategic planning, the plan can be as accurate and effective as you want it to be. Still, strategic planning can be accurate only when it is backed up by thorough and detailed market research.

Market research supports the strategic planning function in a number of ways: it can define existing markets and competition; it can assist in the identification of optimal strategic actions; and it can help in monitoring competitors' activities over the long-run.

Market research serves as the basis for setting objectives. Setting objectives is the basis for planning — if there were no clear-cut objectives, strategic planning would be useless.

Any long-range planning should involve participation by the market research department or the use of external market research or both. In many companies, it is corporate policy for the executives to assemble their long-term plan based on market research data.

The provision of up-to-the-minute market and sales forecasts, and long-range projections for growth of existing and potential technologies, is intrinsic to the planning process.

When it comes to strategic planning, market research is more than a forecasting tool for management. It should be utilized more fully to help attain the company's long-term goals of exploring potential new objectives and alternatives and identifying unexploited markets and product areas.

It should also be among the exclusive responsibilities of the market research function to recommend appropriate strategies and actions required to meet potential goals.

Market Research Options

When considering market research for your business, understand the differences and similarities between your options.

Option 1 – Internal Research

Conducting market research internally may sound like the easiest and most cost-effective research alternative, but this can be both expensive and difficult. For a successful internal research process, all members of your market research group must understand the potential applications and limitations of market research.

A representative of the market research group or, in a small company, the individual responsible for internal market research, should act as liaison between the market research function and company management. Plans of action based on current information should be recommended and requests for additional information made.

In small companies, responsibility for the internal market research function often falls on the vice president of marketing or the president of the company.

Larger corporations generally establish a separate internal market research group which responds to the vice president of marketing. The department may consist of a single research manager or a research manager and several analysts.

Staffing depends on the type of company, its information requirements, and the selected mix between internal and external, or purchased, research.

The organizational structure of the internal research function varies, depending on management's information requirements. Companies not pursuing rapid growth or expansion will generally require less internal research than a company pursuing rapid expansion into new product areas or markets.

The company experiencing market penetration problems and stiff competition will generally structure its internal market research to conduct comprehensive competitive analysis. A company attempting to establish technological leadership will attempt to structure its internal research to ensure comprehensive technology monitoring and forecasting.

In summary, the structure of a company's internal research function is highly dependent on the nature of the company, its goals, objectives, and strategies.

Option 2 – Custom Research

At some point, virtually all internal market research organizations will use external, or purchased, research. These services may be in the form of off-the-shelf or custom (single-client) studies.

The market information required is occasionally far too specific or detailed to be found in an off-the-shelf report. Therefore, your market research budget should include a contingency for purchasing custom market research.

Custom studies are extremely effective in meeting specific information requirements and can be utilized if:

- An off-the-shelf study addressing relevant issues is unavailable;
- The detail contained in available off-the-shelf reports is not sufficient to meet your needs; or
- The research topic is so broad that it requires a mixture of both internal and external consultant staffs for completion.

Option 3 – Off-the-Shelf Research

Off-the-shelf reports are another form of external or purchased market research. These reports are usually broadly based and designed to meet the differing needs and specialties of a number of clients, but do not expect one of these studies to meet all specific information needs.

Multiclient market research offers a number of distinct advantages. As the costs of off-the-shelf research are spread among a number of clients, you can often obtain a completely comprehensive report for a fraction of the cost of funding internal research or purchasing custom consulting services.

In addition, an off-the-shelf report can often be purchased before the end or beginning of research to influence the structure of the research. If you are considering this form of research, Chapter 12 provides a detailed description of off-the-shelf research.

Section 2

The Research

P R O C E S S

Chapter 2

The Internal Research Function

While many firms conduct market research internally, utilizing a specially organized group within their marketing department, various companies have their detailed market research conducted outside the company.

A number of organizations are prepared to meet the market research needs of companies either for a flat fee or on a contract basis. The primary sources of external market research are:

- Market research firms;
- Management consulting groups;
- Independent consultants;
- Advertising agencies;
- University business schools and economic research groups; and
- Trade associations.

For a detailed description of organizations that supply external market research, refer to Chapter 11.

When deciding between conducting research internally or buying it, a number of factors should be considered. The following factors should simplify the decision making process considerably.

- Staff — Does internal staff have the necessary expertise to conduct and complete the research project?

- Equipment — Would an internal research project necessitate acquiring additional equipment, such as additional phones for interview purposes?

- Internal politics — Does the study include any sensitive issues regarding certain departments within the company? For example, does the report rate department efficiency? If so, these types of research projects are best performed externally.

- Administration — Consider the existing pressure and workloads on administrative personnel, and try to determine their capacity to handle additional work arising through the research project.

- Budget — Could an external research project be completed less expensively? This must always be the ultimate consideration in deciding between internal and external research.

- Confidentiality — If confidentiality is the key to the success or failure of the research project, conduct the research externally to minimize the potential for information leaks.

Organizing the Research Process

The organization of the internal research process is dependent on your company's size and organizational structure. Small companies will generally not have a full-time, in-house research staff; an individual is usually responsible for market research duties.

In large companies, organization of the research function becomes more complicated. Although no one form of organization appears to be consistently superior in all situations, certain types of organization appear more workable than others.

The degree of centralization or decentralization within a firm greatly impacts the organization of research. The following methods of research organization are often combined.

- Organization by type of research function performed — For example, product development planning, sales analysis and forecasting, and research into the effects of advertising.

- Organization by technique or method of research used — For example, statistical analysis, questionnaire design, interviewing methodology, and sales analysis.

- Organization by intended use of the research — For example, market segment and product or product line.

If a corporate structure is highly decentralized — as is most often the case in the United States — a number of organizational issues should be considered. Principal organizational considerations for a decentralized firm are as follows:

- Should each department have its own market research group?

- Should a central market research group meet all corporate research needs?

- Should groups be formed at both the corporate and individual department level?

Each alternative offers a variety of advantages, and each must be considered. Adaptability to change is the crucial factor in the organizational structure of the market research function.

The size, organizational structure, and competitive structure of your firm will change over time; the structure of the market research function must be responsive to changing company requirements.

The organizational emphasis of the market research function has shifted considerably in recent years. Rather than being a stop-gap measure used on a problem-solving basis, the trend has now moved to setting up comprehensive market information systems.

Determine Your Goals and Objectives

Before any internal research process begins, it is essential that the project's goals and objectives are clearly identified and stated. All members of the research team need to keep these objectives in mind at all times and work toward the same goal.

When defining the overall goals and objectives, first identify the subparts of the whole process, including:

- Problem definition;

- Research outline creation;

- Data collection method selection;

- Measurement method choice;

- Sample identification; and

- Analysis methodology selection.

Clearly Define the Problem

Identifying your market research problem is half the research battle. By defining the problem, you identify the objectives of the research project and can design the project to meet those objectives.

To identify problems, internal communication between key decision makers and the market research group must be maintained. Before beginning the research project, decision makers should be aware of the practical limitations on the market research group. In addition, the researchers must have a keen understanding of the objectives of the project.

Defining the problem and forming objectives are the keys to any successful project. Your research group must work together with your decision makers to successfully identify the problems. The research group alone should then define the objectives on the basis of the identified problems.

When attempting to identify problems, break the decision making process down to basics, identifying potential problems that may arise from decisions made on an ongoing basis.

Problems arise when there is a goal to reach and alternative ways of reaching that goal exist. Figure 2-1 assists in identifying problems of understanding the decision making situation.

After the research group has a comprehensive understanding of the entire decision making process and the potential results arising through different courses of action, the problems of decision making may become the focus of the research problem.

Figure 2-1
Analyzing the Decision Making Situation

- Assess individual decision makers and their surroundings. Be aware of the tasks frequently facing the decision maker and how he or she approaches these tasks. What resources does he or she have to complete these tasks? In what time frames does he or she generally operate?

- The researcher must be aware of all available options. During the research project certain options will be relayed to the researcher through decision makers. The researcher should ensure that all available options are analyzed.

- The researcher needs to identify the types of decision makers to effectively define the project objectives. Some decision makers are willing to make risky decisions if potential reward exists, while others are not. This can greatly influence his or her style.

- The end result of different alternatives must be addressed. Market research should assess the end result of manipulating various components of the marketing mix to achieve certain goals. The ultimate responsibility of the researcher is to design a research process analyzing the potential outcome of all possible marketing actions.

Decision making problems become the problems of the research project. The two problems are intertwined but are not one and the same. Decision making problems revolve around deciding what has to be achieved. Research problems involve finding the correct information to assist decision makers in making the correct choices.

The fundamental research dilemma lies in determining what information to provide and how to obtain this information. The process of problem definition can be broken down into four steps.

- Step 1 – Discuss problems — Meet with decision makers and discuss their perceptions of the problems. Attempt to determine the accuracy of the manager's perceptions and identify his or her primary concerns for the direction of research. An incorrect management problem related to an incorrect research problem could have disastrous results.

- Step 2 – Focus on the situation — Try to identify all the variables contributing to the management problem. This generally involves a careful analysis of all available company records, industry records, secondary sources, and interviews with company and outside sources.

- Step 3 – Put together possible scenarios — Once you have an understanding of the problems begin to work out scenarios for the manager. These scenarios should take into account management objectives and any variables which could impact these objectives.

- Step 4 – Know how your research will be used — Although the manager can assist in developing scenarios, the researcher should focus on developing the best possible scenario.

Design Your Research Outline

All research projects should begin with an outline process. During the conceptual phase of the project, a first draft outline of market segments, technology, end-users, and competitors should be compiled to help define the scope and objectives of the study.

Refinements to the outline can be made as preliminary research begins, and minor alterations and refinements may continue over the entire course of the research project. A detailed market analysis will likely include:

- An introduction;
- Market analysis/forecasts, including market share information;
- Profiles of competitors;
- A brief executive summary; and
- Conclusions and recommendations.

Organize the outline according to the Roman numeral system. Label major subject divisions with capital letters, topics with lower case letters, and subtopics with numbers. Use good outlining techniques and avoid any stand-alone entries — for every A there must be a B, and so on.

The correct structure for a working market segment section is as follows:

Forecasts of the _____ market

1. Dollar sales
2. Unit sales
3. Growth rate projections
4. Market trends
5. Competitive analysis/market share

The structure of your outline is essential to the success of your research project.

Use the following list of pointers when structuring the research outline.

- From the very start of the research project, it is important for the researcher to discuss the outline contents with the appropriate decision makers.
- The outline should be as detailed and specific as possible. The more detail included in the outline, the better the finished product will meet the needs of decision makers.
- All applicable market segments should be addressed.

- Markets to be analyzed should be segmented according to prevailing industry standards.

- Industry terminology should be used to describe market and product segments.

- The completed outline should be concise. The outline forms the basis for the table of contents.

- Make sure the outline is broken down correctly and the text conforms to it.

Figure 2-2 provides an example of a successful outline.

Select a Data Collection Method

The selection of a data collection method is one of the primary decisions to make in an internal market research project. Three data collection methods are available for market research: primary, secondary, and experimental. The definition, nature, and possible use for each of these methods are discussed at length in Chapter 3.

Instead of selecting only one of these methods, it is worthwhile to use a combination of all three. In many cases it is useful to start the research process with a period of relevant secondary data gathering, then proceed to primary information gathering, which consists of telephone, personal, or mail interviews to acquire more accurate and timely data. Market testing should be utilized to assess a new product or the expansion of the market for an existing product's performance.

Analysts conducting research generally break down the research process in terms of the types of data required. The method of data collection chosen will be influenced by several factors:

- The type of information required;

- The value of the desired information; and

- The judgment of the analyst.

Determine the Measurement Method

Several measurement methods are used in market research. After determining how data will be collected, select the measurement method to use in the research project. Commonly used alternatives include:

- Depth interview and projection methods — These methods are useful in obtaining information respondents might otherwise be unwilling to provide. Projection allows respondents to project their own underlying opinions onto another individual. Depth interviews allow respondents to freely express themselves without interviewer interference.

- Observation methods — These methods rely on direct behavioral examination.

- Questionnaires — These are a means of acquiring information directly from respondents through a carefully designed series of questions.

- Attitude scales — These are a formal research method relying on reports from respondents about a product or market. Types of attitude scales include multidimensional, composite, and rating scales.

Figure 2-2
Research Outline Structure Example

I. Executive Summary
    A. Growing Importance of Private Pay Phones
    B. Market Forecasts and Trends
    C. Technology Developments
    D. Competitive Factors

II. Introduction
    A. Impact of Deregulation and the Federal Communications Commission (FCC)
    B. Public Utility Commission (PUC) and Public Service Commission (PSC) Private Pay phone Tariffs
    C. Importance of Standardization and Answering Supervision
    D. Increasing Owner Education
    E. Target Groups
    F. Lease/Buy Options
    G. Special Feature/Enhancement Trends
        1. Advertising Displays
        2. Drive-Up Pay Phones
        3. Local Calling Only
        4. Recorded Messaging
        5. Smart Pay Phones
        6. Telemessaging
        7. Voice Synthesis
        8. Other Special Features
    H. Improving Industry Reputation
    I. Industry Shake-out

III. Total Private Pay Phone Market Forecasts
    A. Methodology
    B. Total Private Pay Phone Dollar Sales
    C. Total Private Pay Phone Unit Sales
    D. Growth Rate Projections
    E. Overall Market Trends

IV. Market Forecasts and Analysis by Private Pay Phone Equipment Segments
    A. Cash Card Private Pay Phones
        1. Dollar Sales
        2. Unit Sales
        3. Growth Rate Projections
        4. Market Trends
        5. Competitive Analysis

Figure 2-2 (continued)

    B.   Coin-operated Private Pay Phones
        1.   Dollar Sales
        2.   Unit Sales
        3.   Growth Rate Projections
        4.   Market Trends
        5.   Competitive Analysis
    C.   Cordless Table Private Pay Phones
        1.   Dollar Sales
        2.   Unit Sales
        3.   Growth Rate Projections
        4.   Market Trends
        5.   Competitive Analysis
    D.   Credit Card Private Pay Phones
        1.   Dollar Sales
        2.   Unit Sales
        3.   Growth Rate Projections
        4.   Market Trends
        5.   Competitive Analysis
    E.   Portable Desktop Private Pay Phones
        1.   Dollar Sales
        2.   Unit Sales
        3.   Growth Rate Projections
        4.   Market Trends
        5.   Competitive Analysis
    F. Universal Private Pay Phones
        1.   Dollar Sales
        2.   Unit Sales
        3.   Growth Rate Projections
        4.   Market Trends
        5.   Competitive Analysis

V.   Strategies For Success
    A.   Barriers to Entry
        1.   Predatory Marketing Practices
        2.   Monopoly Positions
    B.   Capital Requirements
    C.   RBOC and Independent Telco Business Opportunities
    D.   Strategies Based on Servicing Existing Base
    E.   Strategies Based on Distribution Channels
    F.   Strategies Based on Applications
    G.   Strategies Based on Features/Enhancements

VI. Profiles of Major Companies

Factors influencing the measurement method selection are similar to those affecting data collection method selection. In selecting a measurement method, consideration should be given to the types of information required by decision makers. The relative importance of the information to decision makers should have an impact on the measurement method chosen.

Select a measurement method compatible with the chosen data collection method and your sample requirements. Since all characteristics of research design are related, ongoing consideration of all aspects of their interaction is essential.

Identify the Sample

Although a sample is a subsegment of a total population group, the sample should not represent a census of the entire population. A good sample consists of a carefully selected segment of the total population deemed representative for the research project. In market research, the sample may be a group of potential end-users, competitors, or distributors.

The sampling process must interact with all other segments of the research process. Primary factors to consider when defining the sample population are:

- Discover who can best answer questions pertaining to the research project.
- Identify the basis for sample selection.
- Determine the size of the desired sample.
- Develop a detailed plan for contacting the selected sample.

Choose an Analysis Methodology

Data analysis involves relating what has been observed to the problem, or simply describing it. The type of analysis completed depends on the data, measurement methods, and sampling processes used. The analysis method should be selected before beginning data collection.

It is often advisable to test a potential analysis method using invented data. This artificial data should be measured using the selected measurement method, then analyzed using the chosen method of analysis to determine if it will adequately address the issues deemed important to decision makers.

Carrying out this test run can prevent the research project from failing to meet the needs of decision makers.

Budgeting Considerations

All companies, large or small, should allocate some portion of their annual budget to market research. This amount will vary based on company size, prevailing management styles, and objectives.

Generally, companies that have competed in mature markets for significant periods of time and are content with stable profit and market growth spend a minimal amount on market research. Companies attempting to expand at a rapid rate, either by increasing profits and market growth rates or by entering new markets through merger and acquisition, spend significant amounts on market research.

Long-term market competitors and many new companies often rely heavily on salespeople for market information; market research is often an integral part of these salespersons' long-term responsibilities.

Developing sales personnel who can successfully conduct market research is a long-term process. If your firm does not have the time or facilities to develop a field sales force capable of conducting ongoing market research via customer feedback, you can either develop a separate in-house market research team, or utilize outside services.

Know the Cost Elements

Once the internal research process has been organized, it is important to determine the resources required to complete the project.

Market research resources are generally considered in terms of the time required to complete the project, and the demands placed on available human resources and equipment. Time and budgetary considerations are closely related.

Total costs of the market research function can be divided into groups of distinct elements:

- Direct staff costs, including:
  - Payroll
  - Other expenses
- Indirect staff costs, including:
  - Management, administrative and other personnel contributing to the research project
- Purchased data costs, including:
  - Multiclient reports
  - Trade press
  - Books, magazines, and other reference materials
  - Information acquired from trade associations

The ideal mix of these components depends on the nature of the internal research project and the company conducting the research.

Long-term competitors in stable markets attempting to encourage ongoing improvements in their product line and enhance their market share growth should consider developing a larger, broadly-based research team.

If the company has competed in a series of markets for a long period of time, the market research group can become experts in their areas, accumulating significant knowledge and building comprehensive databases. Significant understanding of existing competition can be acquired over time and forecasting methodologies refined and perfected.

Review Your Business' Objective

When organizing your research project, one of the first tasks should be to review the strategic goals and objectives of your company.

- Is your business dynamic and innovative?
- Are you trying to diversify and expand into new markets?

- Is merger and acquisition part of your business' expansion strategy?

- Is yours a stable company?

- Is the company a long-term competitor in a given series of market segments with a goal of expanding its share of these markets over time and enhancing profits?

Business type influences the structure of the research program and the comparative costs of the project. Reevaluate your business, its existing goals and objectives; structure the research project accordingly.

Start by putting together an outline focusing on your company and its objectives. Subsequent evaluation of this outline will remind you of the parameters you should place on the research project.

As an understanding of the time and financial requirements of the research project develops, the balance between internal, external, and purchased research will become increasingly clear. Following are reasons for considering the use of purchased information.

Identifying an Optimal Mix

- The need for research information may fluctuate widely from period to period.

- Sudden death or crash projects may require data faster than the in-house staff can complete the project.

- The project may create a short-term need for knowledge and expertise the company's research group does not have.

Any internal research budgeting program should examine available multi-client reports addressing the issues the internal group needs to analyze. Calculate the costs of performing the research in-house and compare those costs.

High quality multiclient studies are available. While they often represent a cost-effective alternative to internal or custom research, they may not meet your specific information requirements, since they are often directed at a general audience with a broad range of interests.

Notes

Chapter 3

Market Research Sources: Primary Versus Secondary Data

Data collected for market research may be divided into separate categories as primary or secondary data.

Secondary research is used to gain an initial insight into the research problem; it is useful in familiarizing the research analyst with industry technology, potential product applications, and (perhaps most importantly) industry terminology and jargon.

Primary research is used to bring the project into focus with specific, timely, and detailed information. When forecasting markets and technology, primary data is particularly valuable for gaining a more detailed insight into the workings of the marketplace.

Introduction

Secondary data is information gathered for purposes other than the completion of the research project. A variety of secondary information sources is available to the researcher accumulating data on certain companies within a particular industry. These data sources will often yield information regarding market share, trends within the industry, and overall industry size.

Secondary data is most effectively classified in terms of its source — either internal or external. Internal, or in-house data, is secondary information acquired within the organization where research is being carried out. External secondary data is obtained from outside sources.

Secondary Market Research – Definition and Role

Internal secondary data is usually an inexpensive information source for the company conducting research. Internally generated sales and pricing data

First Type – Internal Secondary Data

can be utilized as a potential research source. The use of this information is generally restricted to research attempting to define the competitive position of the firm or the evaluation of a marketing strategy the firm has used in the past.

The role of internal secondary data in determining future marketing decisions or industry direction is limited. There are three basic sources for this type of data:

- Sales and market reports;

- Accounting/financial records; and

- Miscellaneous records.

Sales and marketing records can be maintained in several ways, including:

- Type of product purchased;

- Type of end-user/industry segment;

- Method of payment;

- Product or product line;

- Sales territory;

- Salesperson;

- Date of purchase;

- Amount of purchase;

- Price;

- Application of product; and

- Location of end-user.

Internal data is an easily acquired, inexpensive source of information. Many businesses do not organize and collect all the data available to them from the marketing department. Frequently, large, diverse companies cannot produce simple sales reports because of poor record organization.

Your business can compile sales and marketing reports relative to:

- Sales by day/month/year;

- Sales by region, salesperson, or territory;

- Sales by customer, product, or application;

- Sales by product over time;

- Advertising expenses;

- Sales quote report;

- Sales call reports;

- Telemarketing reports; or

- Public relations reports.

Accounting records, an often overlooked source of internal secondary information, can be invaluable in the identification, clarification, and prediction of certain problems.

Accounting and financial information systems are typically the most organized and detailed information systems a business has. The only drawback to these systems is the timeliness factor — it is often several months before accounting statements are ready.

Potentially, this information can be applied to measure sales effectiveness by analyzing various marketing expenses over a period of time. For example, the cost of a direct mail campaign for a certain product can be compared to the resulting sales. Don't hesitate to provide in-house researchers with:

- Income statements,
- Sources and users of funds,
- Accounts payable, and
- Expenses over time.

Although a great deal of the information gathered from financial, accounting, and miscellaneous reports (such as inventory, service, personnel, production, and research and development reports) does not fall under traditional market research areas, it can be a critical source for evaluating and comparing your company to industry or competitor performance.

Second Type – External Secondary Data

External secondary data may be acquired from a variety of sources. Vast quantities of published external secondary data are available to the analyst and can facilitate the research effort. While more costly and time consuming to acquire than internal secondary data, external secondary information can provide more valuable data for a market analysis.

The primary sources of external secondary data are:

- Government agencies,
- Associations,
- Computerized bibliographies,
- Syndicated services, and
- Other published sources.

Government Agencies. Government bodies at the federal, state, and local levels produce vast quantities of pertinent market research data. The major agencies within the federal government responsible for accumulating and distributing statistical information are:

- National Center for Health Statistics;
- Bureau of the Census;
- Statistical Reporting Service, Department of Agriculture;
- Bureau of Labor Statistics; and
- National Center for Educational Statistics.

In addition to a variety of regulatory and administrative agencies that produce industry-related reports on a regular basis, a great number of specialized government research and analysis groups exists.

Associations. Associations publish information on sales, growth trends, product development, and company performance within the industry. Information acquired by the associations may be published as annual reports, trade journals, or special limited reports. The majority of libraries contain references listing associations and their related activities.

Computerized Bibliographies/Commercial Databases. Use of computerized databases has increased in both prevalence and depth in recent years. Use of commercial databases requires access to a computer terminal and modem. Large quantities of secondary data can be retrieved in a comparatively short time period.

National Technical Information Service (NTIS). NTIS is a computerized bibliography service providing acquisition of secondary data for market research purposes. Other potentially useful commercial databases include Abstracted Business Information (ABI/INFORM), Predicast Terminal System, and Management Contents.

Syndicated Services. A number of syndicated services are also available to market researchers. Numerous firms in the United States collate, package, and distribute information on a subscription basis. Data provided by these syndicated services may be broken down into three separate categories, including:

- Data on product movement through retailers;

- Data on product movement through wholesalers; and

- Data on the reactions of end-users and consumers to marketing strategies.

Syndicated data also includes public opinion polls such as those conducted by Gallup, Inc. These polls can provide indications of variations in end-user behavior patterns. Omnibus surveys also fall into the syndicated service category. Since the agency producing the omnibus survey often inserts questions of relevance to certain clients, this type of survey becomes primary data generated to address the specific research issue at hand.

Other Published Sources. A seemingly endless collection of periodicals, newspapers, reports, and books contain secondary data relevant to the market research function. To list and describe even the more important of these sources is beyond the scope of this manual.

Secondary Data and the Research Process

A basic secondary source can answer, or at least address, some of your fundamental research issues. Secondary research can help you better define research issues and formulate potential hypotheses on how to most effectively address the problem.

Articles, trade directories, Department of Commerce information, and other secondary sources will only point you in the right direction. It is unlikely that all answers to research questions will be found in the secondary research stage.

The two major advantages of secondary data are time and cost savings.

Advantages of Secondary Data

The secondary research process can be completed rapidly —generally in two to three weeks. Substantial useful secondary information can be assembled by a skilled analyst in two to three days.

When secondary data is readily available, the researcher need only locate the source or sources of the data and extract the required information. Therefore, secondary data can be assembled quickly, allowing the analyst to gain an overall picture of the relevant market.

Secondary research is generally less expensive than primary research. The bulk of secondary research data gathering does not require the use of expensive, specialized, highly trained personnel.

Secondary research expenses are generally incurred by the originator of the information. The burden of these expenses is spread out among a number of users and represents a substantially lower investment than initially obtaining and packaging the data.

Secondary data may not address your business' specific research issues. Most users find their area of interest so specific that the data is either too general to be useful, or is nonexistent. The following factors outline the principal disadvantages of secondary research.

Disadvantages of Secondary Data

Availability. Secondary information pertinent to the research topic is either not available, or is only available in insufficient quantities.

Accuracy and Reliability. An analyst must determine the accuracy of secondary research data before beginning to assemble reliable market data.

It is frequently more difficult to assess the accuracy of secondary research data than that of primary data. When determining the accuracy of secondary information, consider the:

- Source of the information;
- Purpose of data publication;
- General quality of the publication; and
- Methodology used to collect the data.

The accuracy of secondary data is critical in the market research industry. An analyst or a company will frequently use secondary data as a basis for marketing decisions, assuming that if the data is printed in a respected publication, it is accurate.

Secondary data in print is often far from accurate or reliable. For example, the highly respected U.S. Department of Commerce publishes trade statistics every year. If analyzed methodically, the ambiguity in product classification systems would make the statistics virtually valueless.

Another inaccurate source of statistics is published annually by trade magazines. These respected publications survey their readers to derive estimates of market size, market growth rate, and purchasing patterns, then average the results. These statistics are merely averaged opinions. Typically, less than 10 percent of the subscriber base responds to these surveys.

Before basing any marketing decisions or analysis on secondary data, investigate the source and the methodology used in collecting the data.

Relevancy. Three primary factors that may be used to assess the relevancy of secondary information to the research topic are:

- Measurement units,

- Definition of classes, and

- Publication date (timeliness).

Available secondary information may be expressed in units different from those the analyst considers appropriate for the project. For example, manufacturing facilities may be described in several ways, including square footage of the facility, number of employees, and production capacity in units or volume.

Class definition can also pose a problem affecting the relevancy of secondary information. For example, if a manufacturer produces a product it feels is best suited to a certain market segment, available secondary data may assess product acceptance in other market segments and minimize the relevance of available data.

Data must be current. Unfortunately, most secondary information is outdated; it may be one to two years old by the time you receive it. Virtually all market research projects require a more accurate picture of the market today.

Above all else, market research must be timely. Trade journals and other published secondary information sources often accept articles for publication six months before they appear in print. While relevant articles may appear in a monthly or weekly magazine, they may have been written much earlier and the research carried out many months before.

In addition to a lack of availability, accuracy, and relevancy, gaps exist in available secondary data because writers generally focus on a small section of the total area researched.

Collecting, sorting, and interpreting mass quantities of secondary literature can often prove difficult, time-consuming, and frustrating, particularly when the researcher wishes to address specific issues.

Consider the Costs of the Sources

Cost and time economies are among the principal advantages of secondary data. However, depending on the source, extent, and depth of the research topic, comprehensive secondary research can prove both costly and time-consuming.

Relative costs of data acquisitions vary from one source to another. Although data may be acquired inexpensively, relevant secondary data may be expensive if you use on-line databases.

The time needed to acquire secondary data can add significantly to the costs of your research project. You must invest extra labor to organize and order secondary data, evaluate its content, and address the issues.

Associations. Information from associations is generally published in annual reports or as part of a regular trade journal. Numerous reference libraries contain the *Encyclopedia of Associations* and other publications listing trade associations and their related areas of interest.

The cost of acquiring secondary data from associations may be divided into two separate categories: labor costs and time costs.

- **Labor.** Knowledgeable researchers must be used to scan libraries for the most appropriate associations, contact the associations, and identify appropriate secondary data. Thus, labor costs associated with the acquisition of secondary information from associations are an important consideration.

- **Time.** The time taken to adequately utilize association data is also an important component of overall secondary data costs.

Commercial Databases. Computer databases require access to a computer terminal and modem. To access the information, you will be charged an initial connection fee, plus a time-based fee of $2 to $3 per minute. A good researcher can often obtain useful secondary information within two hours.

Syndicated Services. Syndicated services are among the more expensive secondary data sources. The U.S. companies that collate and package secondary data pass on the costs of data collection and packaging to you — the ultimate user. So the expense involved in obtaining the information is often considerable.

Government Agencies. Government agencies are among the most inexpensive of all potential data sources. Some data is provided by government agencies free or for a minimal charge. Because the information is usually dated, you must take a great deal of time evaluating government data, which can add considerably to the time/labor expense involved in secondary data research.

Other Published Sources. Researchers will find numerous published data sources ranging from general magazine articles to detailed market research studies. These sources can fluctuate in cost from a few dollars to $1,500 or more for a comprehensive, off-the-shelf market study.

The time and labor required to identify existing resources must be considered potential costs. Costs of the secondary research process can accumulate rapidly in a number of areas. The worksheet in Figure 3-1 will enable your company to effectively estimate its potential secondary research costs by the source of secondary research it chooses. The commercial database section has been partially completed as an example of potential costs.

Formulating a Secondary Research Methodology

There is often a tendency to gather large amounts of information at the start of a secondary research information search. A frequently encountered problem is that the researcher devotes little or no time to assembling a comprehensive research methodology to effectively organize the research acquired.

You may experience confusion, added effort, and frustration if you lack a methodology in secondary data management. You can avoid this by creating a general strategy for completing the secondary research phase, focusing on the initial data collection and sorting processes. This initial stage should be completed before locating secondary data sources.

It is important to consider:

- What information is being sought?
- How will data be sorted?
- What sources will be used?

After answering these questions, you can begin to compile secondary information.

Know Your Objectives

Secondary research is a necessary component of the market research process. You should use secondary data before and during the primary research phase to identify potential primary sources and gain improved insight into the research problem. Secondary research is valuable in defining an industry population and identifying a required sample size for the primary research phase of the project.

Your main objective in secondary research is to familiarize yourself with important industry factors such as technology, general product applications, market suppliers, terminology unique to the marketplace, and an overview of the market.

In short, the goal of secondary research is to provide you, as the researcher, with an inexpensive way to understand the broad perspective of the market.

Categorizing Secondary Data

As an effective analyst, you need to focus on specific goals and objectives to avoid confusion and wasted effort. To look for "any information concerning the industry" is too broad an objective; specific topics should be addressed during the secondary data gathering stage.

Formulate a specific list detailing the categories for collecting and organizing secondary information, as an aid to simplifying data evaluation and utilization.

Then, you can formulate general impressions and identify relevant issues and competitors once secondary data relating to topics on the list have been accumulated.

Figure 3-1
Worksheet to Determine Potential Secondary Data Costs

1. Labor Costs (e.g., terminal operator hourly wage) $ 8.00
2. Information Acquisition Costs
    (e.g., database connection fee) $150.00
3. Time Costs per Minute
    (e.g., time based fee for data base use) $2.00-$3.00
4. Equipment Costs
    (e.g., computer terminal and modem) $1,000.00
5. Total costs $_____

Associations
1. Labor Costs $_____
2. Information Acquisition Costs $_____
3. Time Costs $_____
4. Equipment Costs $_____
5. Total Costs $_____

Government Agencies
1. Labor Costs $_____
2. Information Acquisition Costs $_____
3. Time Costs $_____
4. Equipment Costs $_____
5. Total Costs $_____

Syndicated Services
1. Labor Costs $_____
2. Information Acquisition Costs $_____
3. Time Costs $_____
4. Equipment Costs $_____
5. Total Costs $_____

Other Published Sources
1. Labor Costs $_____
2. Information Acquisition Costs $_____
3. Time Costs $_____
4. Equipment Costs $_____
5. Total Costs $_____

Next, conduct a review to determine exactly what data is there and which categories have been covered. For example, secondary information obtained may be categorized by product, competitor, general industry, and market. Be sure sufficient information has been collected for each category. Figure 3-2 provides an example of a list categorizing secondary information.

Secondary information from published sources should be carefully examined for results during the analysis. Once you have developed an impression of market magnitudes, then develop a primary research strategy. The secondary data you uncover may change the nature of the primary research stage from trend identification to trend exploration.

Figure 3-2
Proposed List Structure for Categorizing
Secondary Data

Product Line Information
    Product Specifications and Comparisons
    Substitute Products
    Complementary products
    Pricing
    Performance

Market Information
    Market Size
    Growth Patterns
    Growth Rates
    Market Share
    Market Maturity

Technology Information
    New Competing Technologies
    Research and Development Efforts
    Rate of Innovation

Market Competitor Information
    Identifying Competitors
    Competitors' Strategies
    Weaknesses and Strengths
    Market Share
    Product Line

Sources for Primary Interviews
    Associations
    Key Company Planners
    Magazines
    Newsletters

Political, Legal, and Social Factors Influencing the Market

The Macroeconomic Environment

Checklist development is vital in the use of secondary research. The list of secondary information you compiled at the beginning of the project should be used to check off data as it is acquired and used.

When conducting and utilizing secondary research, the most important factor to remember is don't overdo it. A frequent mistake is that the analyst spends a great deal of time accumulating masses of secondary information hoping to find specific answers to research questions.

Remember, secondary data provides a basic working knowledge of the industry. Therefore, don't exhaust all available secondary information sources before starting the primary research phase. Primary and secondary research should proceed concurrently, with one feeding the other.

The most common failure of internal and corporate market research staff is over-reliance on secondary market research. It is very easy to simply review secondary information.

How to Use Secondary Data

The analyst has now defined secondary research objectives, developed a framework for gathering the information, and is ready to begin collecting secondary data.

Depending on the overall estimated length of the research project (assume that total project length is ten weeks), the analyst should not allocate more than 20 percent of total project time to secondary research. Typically, the secondary research stage lasts two weeks. Uses of secondary data information include:

- Preliminary analysis;
- Analysis for results;
- Checklist development;
- Structuring the primary research process; and
- Identifying primary research sources.

Alternate methods of data compilation are by year, company, and function.

Once secondary data has been gathered and categorized, you can begin to use the data to make observations and form opinions. Secondary data may be divided into three stages of analysis:

- Gather, read, and sort industry information;
- Gather company-specific information; and
- Write an industry and technology background.

Four Key Segments of the Research Project

The market research process may be divided into four distinct segments — industry overview data, industry financial data, management profile data, and historical competitor data. To gather the appropriate data for each segment, it is important that you use the proper information sources for each.

Segment 1 – Industry Overview Data

Certain sources may be considered optimal when compiling a general industry overview using secondary information. Typical sources of industry overview data are:

- Annual issues of trade magazines,
- *The Wall Street Transcript*,
- Market research studies,
- U.S. Department of Commerce, and
- Commercial databases.

Annual Issues of Trade Magazines. The majority of major trade journals and magazines devote an issue annually to an industry review. The subjects addressed in these reviews include primary industry players, sales volume, and general market information.

The Wall Street Transcript. This publication can provide the analyst with detailed company-specific secondary information, in addition to reviews on the entire industry. The broad-based emphasis of this newspaper can provide the researcher with an excellent grasp of general industry trends and issues.

Market Studies. Market studies are available from a variety of sources. Reports furnished by publishing houses, stock analysts, and market research firms often provide the analyst with a useful general overview of the industry.

U.S. Department of Commerce. The U.S. Department of Commerce is responsible for compiling data on industry trends and shipments. Annual reports produced by the agency include the *U.S. Industrial Outlook Handbook* and *Current Industrial Reports*.

Commercial Databases. These databases collate market data from many sources, compiling the data in statistical form or as text or both. The information is usually quite broad but it may be useful in developing an industry overview.

Segment 2 – Industry Financial Data

Secondary information sources can provide industry financial data. Some of the optimal financial data sources are:

- Trade association publications;
- Government reports;
- *The Wall Street Transcript;*
- Trade news articles;
- *Moody's Investors Manual;* and
- Industry directories.

Segment 3 – Management Profile Data

Profiles of key management personnel in leading industries are occasionally necessary. You can use a variety of secondary information sources to assemble these profiles. Prime sources to research include:

- Who's Who directories;

- Dun and Bradstreet reports;

- Annual reports and proxy;

- Local newspapers; and

- Industry directories.

Historical information on competing firms can be helpful in compiling profiles of industry competitors. The primary sources of necessary information are:

- Annual reports;

- Trade news and special reports;

- Company annual reports;

- SEC filings;

- Case studies (summaries of company operations provided by university business schools);

- *Moody's Investors Manual;* and

- Company product literature.

Segment 4 – Historical Competitor Data

Vast amounts of secondary data are available to researchers for industry analysis. The volume of published secondary information available varies by industry.

Figure 3-3 provides an example of potential secondary information sources in the electronics industry and how to effectively categorize data by source. The listing is not complete, but should provide a good indication of likely sources for a data search.

A General Guide to Secondary Data Sources

Figure 3-3
General Business Secondary Information Sources

Periodicals
Advertising Age
Crain Communications, Inc.
220 East 42nd Street
New York, NY 10017-5846
(212) 210-0100

Barron's National Business & Financial Weekly
Dow Jones & Company, Inc.
200 Liberty Street
New York, NY 10281-1003
(212) 416-2700

American Demographics
American Demographics, Inc.
PO Box 68
Ithaca, NY 14851
(800) 828-1133

Business Week
McGraw-Hill, Inc.
1221 Avenue of the Americas
New York, NY 10020-1001
(212) 512-6839

Forbes
Forbes, Inc.
60 Fifth Avenue
New York, NY 10011-8865
(212) 620-2200

Fortune
Time, Inc.
Time/Life Building
New York, NY 10020
(212) 522-1212

International Financial Statistics
International Monetary Fund
19th and "H" Streets, NW
Washington, DC 20431
(202) 623-7430

Figure 3-3 (continued)

International Management
Reed Business Publishing
205 East 42nd Street
New York, NY 10017
(212) 867-2080

Nation's Business
Chamber of Commerce of the United States
1615 "H" Street, NW
Washington, DC 20062-2000
(202) 463-5650

Wall Street Journal
Dow Jones & Company, Inc.
200 Liberty Street
New York, NY 10281-1099
(212) 416-2000

The Wall Street Transcript
Wall Street Transcript, Inc.
99 Wall Street, 22nd Floor
New York, NY 10005-4393
(212) 747-9500

Indexes, Abstracts and Bibliographies
Business Periodicals Index
HW Wilson Company
950 University Ave.
Bronx, NY 10452
(800) 367-6770

F & S Index United States
Predicasts, Inc.
11001 Cedar Avenue
Cleveland, OH 44106
(800) 321-6388

New York Times Index
The New York Times
229 West 43rd Street
New York, NY 10036
(212) 556-1573

Figure 3-3 (continued)

Wall Street Journal Index
Dow Jones & Company, Inc.
P.O. Box 300
Princeton, NJ 08543-0300
(609) 520-4000

Directories, Guides and Reference Works
American Survey of Manufacturers
Bureau of the Census
Industry Division
Room 2102 Bldg. 4
Washington, DC 20233
(301) 763-7304

CEDDS: The Complete Economic and Demographic Data Source
Woods & Poole Economics, Inc.
1794 Columbus Road NW, Ste. 4
Washington, DC 20009-2805
(800) 786-1915

Cendata
Bureau of the Census
Washington, DC 20233
(301) 763-7682

Corporate Finance Sourcebook
National Register Publishing
121 Chanlon Road
New Providence, NJ 07974
(800) 521-8118

Dun & Bradstreet Directories
Dun & Bradstreet Information Services
3 Sylvan Way
Parsippany, NJ 07054
(800) 526-0651

The Encyclopedia of Associations
Gale Research, Inc.
835 Penobscot Building
Detroit, MI 48226
(800) 877-4253

Figure 3-3 (continued)

Irwin Business and Investment Almanac
Irwin Professional Publishing
1333 Burr Ridge Pkwy.
Burr Ridge, IL 60521
(800) 634-3966

Moody's Industrial Manual and *Moody's Manuals*
Moody's Investor Services
Dun & Bradstreet Corporation
99 Church Street
New York, NY 10007
(800) 342-5647 ext. 0546

Standard and Poor's Register of Corporations: Directories & Executives
Standard & Poor's
25 Broadway
New York, NY 10004
(800) 852-1641

Standard Corporation Descriptions
Standard & Poor's Corporation
25 Broadway
New York, NY 10004
(800) 852-1641

Ulrich's International Periodicals Directory
121 Chanlon Road
New Providence, NJ 07974
(800) 821-8110

Newsletters
Directory of Investment Research
Nelson Publications
One Gateway Plaza
Portchester, NY 10573
(914) 937-8400

The Boomer Report
FIND/SVP
625 Avenue of the Americas
New York, NY 10011
(800) 346-3787

Figure 3-3 (continued)

Government Publications
Government Research Directory
Gale Research, Inc.
835 Penobscot Building
Detroit, MI 48226
(800) 877-4253

Guide to NIST
Institute of Standards & Technology
Bldg. 101, Room A47
Gaithersburg, MD 20899
(301) 975-3058

NTIS Products and Services Catalog
National Technical Information Service
International Trade Administration
5385 Port Royal Road
Springfield, VA 22161
(703) 487-4650

Researching Markets, Industries and Business Opportunities
Washington Researchers
2612 "P" Street, NW
Washington, DC 20007
(202) 333-3533

Survey of Current Business
Superintendent of Documents
Mail Stop SM
Washington, DC 20402
(202) 512-2250

Primary Market Research — Definition and Role

Primary data is required information generated by an analyst to complete a research project. Accurate primary research is required when:

- Secondary (published) information is not available;
- Research is focused on a specific topic rather than a general one;
- Accurate detailed competitive information is required;
- Detailed forecasting and technology analysis is required; or
- The market being researched is new rather than mature.

Likely sources of primary industry information include:

- Outside industry observers, such as:
  - Unions
  - Press groups
  - Local chambers of commerce
  - Government groups
  - Financial organizations
  - Regulatory agencies
- Company industry sources, such as:
  - Sales force
  - Service group
  - Engineering group
  - Purchasing group
  - Market research staff
  - Research and development
- Service groups, such as:
  - Trade associations
  - Investment banks
  - Commercial banks
  - Advertising corporations
  - Industry consultants
  - Auditors

Primary research — obtaining current data directly from manufacturers, end-users, distributors, and other market participants — is vital for developing accurate, real-time analyses of expected growth for specific products and technologies. As an analyst, you must utilize primary data to ensure accuracy and consistency.

Secondary research rarely provides an adequate solution to a market research problem. Measurement units or classes or both, used in reporting data, are often incorrect; the data may be obsolete when published, or available secondary data may be incomplete.

Primary data collection represents the most important phase of the information gathering process. This phase should represent approximately 80 percent of the research process. Ideally, primary research should be conducted simultaneously with the secondary research stage. The essential goal of the primary research stage should be to:

- Establish project goals and information needs;
- Project a timeframe;

Primary Data and the Research Process

Formulating a Primary Research Methodology

- Identify the current base year marketplace for the product;

- Forecast market growth;

- Acquire data for competitive analysis; and

- Formulate technology forecasts and assess potential impact on demand and product characteristics.

Categorizing Primary Data

Before beginning the primary research stage, the entire segment of the project should be outlined in significant detail. Categorizing objectives and methods will ensure that you receive the required information within the allotted time and cost constraints.

Early planning and organization of primary research may require as much as 10 percent of total primary research process time — an initial investment of time that saves difficulty later. The primary research project plan should include:

- Primary research methodology;

- Time constraints;

- Budget constraints;

- Objective — What information is to be obtained?

- Management — Who will direct the process? What human resources are available? and

- Support staff.

The organization of the primary research phase should be detailed in writing. Specific elements you want to include in primary research must be clearly identified. This early planning may be worth two days of your time. The following key elements in the primary research planning phase should be outlined.

- Forecast period — How long is the forecast period? Does each year in the period need to be forecast?

- Quantification method — What should be included in the forecast? Will the forecast address dollar and unit sales? Will pricing considerations be included?

- Market product segments — Identify potential markets and note all product applications, including market application segments, end-user segments, and geographic segments.

- Technological developments — Identify the fields of technology to be analyzed.

- Competitive analysis — Consider the number of competitors to analyze and exactly what competitor information is required. Detailed market share information, product development trends, and pricing strategies of major competitors should be listed.

- End-user information — Types of end-user data required should be specified in detail to avoid any ambiguity during the primary research stage.

Primary data should be used to develop a current picture of industry performance. Primary data is the most effective way to assemble market forecasts, competitor information, technical and product development trends, and product pricing information. You can effectively use primary data to:

- Solve the research objective;

- Identify problems;

- Address specific questions and issues;

- Apply quality control standards to the research outline;

- Identify new market trends as they occur; and

- Confirm whether all industry competitors or potential competitors are being addressed.

How to Use Primary Data

Survey research involves gathering information from a group of respondents for improving understanding or predicting certain behavioral aspects within the market or industry. Interviews provide the main source of information in the primary research process. There are three basic interview methods, each with its own particular advantages, disadvantages, and ideal application areas. Primary interview survey techniques include:

- Personal interviews,

- Telephone interviews, and

- Mail surveys.

Surveys – The Primary Data Gathering Source

Specific information requirements — information that competing methods can provide — and time and budgetary constraints will determine which approach to use.

One of your primary considerations is to decide which method of administration can provide the required information from the sample group at the lowest cost.

Personal interviews are generally the most expensive method of survey administration. Telephone interviewing is slightly more expensive than mail surveying unless phone interviews are kept short.

Another key consideration is choosing a primary data collection method. Sometimes the method choice implies a variety of supplementary decisions, such as whether the questionnaire should be disguised or undisguised, structured or unstructured. Overall, you will want to be concerned with the primary issues of questionnaire design, administration, and the analysis of incoming data.

You may select a mail survey if:

- A considerable number of potential data sources exist with readily available names and addresses; and

- The required information can be attained through the use of a questionnaire.

Survey Option 1 – Mail Questionnaires

Mail survey questionnaires are sent to potential respondents with a more than passing familiarity with the research issue or topic. The questionnaire should be sent with a letter of introduction that clearly explains the survey objectives and asks the respondent to complete and return the survey.

Mail surveys are particularly useful in substantiating perceived trends. Mail questionnaires can prove a useful link to other forms of primary research, particularly for determining desirable product features and as a product design guide. They provide both qualitative and quantitative primary data from large or widely dispersed population samples and are preferable to telephone surveys if:

- The sample required is very large and the budget limited;

- The information sought is not excessively detailed; or

- The information sought is quantitative rather than qualitative.

Mail Survey Advantages. One survey method of primary data collection is not consistently superior to another. The type of information desired and existing time and budget constraints will determine the method selected. The main advantages of using mail surveys in primary data gathering are:

- Interviewer bias is avoided.

- Sample size is increased, thus improving accuracy.

- Broad geographic areas are covered.

- Anonymity available to the respondent can result in interesting and valuable information.

- Wide distribution can be achieved at a comparatively low cost.

- A number of data processing alternatives are open; computer checks and cross checks can be easily performed.

Mail Survey Disadvantages. Market research questionnaires, however, are generally plagued by a variety of disadvantages. For mail survey findings to be valid, statistical sampling techniques must be valid. The premise of the mail survey is that the group of end-users or competitors is homogeneous and large. An appropriate questionnaire must be designed and a sample, representative of the entire population of end-users of the product, must complete the questionnaire.

Statistical analysis can then be used to draw conclusions about the product, based on the representative sample. For effective statistical analysis, a significant number of responses are required. Typically, responses vary between 1 and 5 percent.

Mail interviews are generally the least flexible interview alternative, and questionnaire complexity seriously affects mail surveys. Questions must be presented to the interviewee in an established order, and all respondents receive identical instructions regardless of their area of expertise. This may enhance the standardization of response, but may also lead to respondent confusion, discouraging participation or distorting results.

Many have questioned the accuracy of data from mail surveys. Unlike respondents in personal or phone interviews, those participating in mail surveys are unable to seek clarification regarding confusing issues or poorly structured questions. Therefore, mail surveys offer the greatest potential for respondent confusion. The mail survey respondent can read the entire questionnaire before answering any questions and can change earlier answers, reducing spontaneity and the presence of potentially revealing answers.

In addition, the responsibilities of an individual within a company are not always clear according to job title. So even if you have a good company mailing list, it is difficult to determine the appropriate survey recipients. A mailing addressed to a specific individual or position title may not reach the person best qualified to respond to the survey.

Another major disadvantage of gathering survey primary data by mail is that these surveys take the most time to complete; there is little you can do to shorten the time period involved. Depending on the survey, it takes at least five weeks before most responses to the first mailing begin to appear. Keep in mind the following drawbacks of mail surveys as a primary data gathering technique.

- Response rates are often disappointing — good response rates vary between 3 and 11 percent.

- Questionnaire length must be limited.

- It is time-consuming to formulate questionnaires, organize mailings, and analyze the responses. It often takes up to five weeks for a response.

- Identifying relevant mailing lists can prove time-consuming and costly.

- Bias can be extensive; respondents often have personal motivation for responding.

- A large respondent base is necessary to ensure an accurate sample.

Mail Survey Cost Considerations. The many potential costs of mail surveys should be considered. Factors to consider when weighing the costs of mail surveys include:

- Type of interview (level of detail);

- Type of questionnaire;

- Required response rate;

- Geographic area to be covered; and

- Time span for the survey.

Cost considerations in selecting any survey must include the cost of making initial contacts and the cost of callbacks and remailings to enhance the rate of response. These cost considerations reveal that mail surveys can be extremely costly, depending on the required sample.

The most significant potential cost of a mail survey is the development of a mailing list. Mailing lists can be acquired from a number of sources if an in-house mailing list is beyond the scope of your business. Since most outside sources will conduct the mailing for you rather than provide you with their list, your control over the mailing is reduced.

The majority of trade periodicals will arrange mailings to their subscribers for a fee. The lists are generally coded by area and job title so you can select an appropriate sample. The primary costs associated with the mail survey method include:

- Mailing list costs (development costs or rental fee). Costs begin at about $70 per thousand names and may range from $50 to $125;

- Questionnaire and cover letter preparation costs;

- Mailing costs (including self-addressed, stamped envelopes and follow-up mailings);

- Gift costs, if gifts are provided as an incentive for the respondent to complete the survey;

- Statistical analysis formulation for use in survey processing;

- Telephone follow-up costs; and

- Data processing costs.

The worksheet in Figure 3-4 will enable you to figure your mail survey costs using cost considerations and factors listed above.

Survey Option 2 – Telephone Interviews

This primary information gathering technique has become more widespread over the past two decades due to the increased use of the telephone and rising costs of personal interviews.

Traditionally, telephone interviews are shorter than either personal or mail interviews. Telephone interviews are generally 15 minutes or less in length, although successful interviews of over an hour are common.

Telephone interviews are more flexible than mail surveys but generally not as flexible as personal interviews. Simplified questionnaires are essential for telephone interviews because the respondent cannot be physically seen to determine if the instructions are truly understood.

Telephone Interview Advantages. Gathering primary data by telephone is the most efficient way to contact a large group of respondents. During a telephone interview, a respondent can easily seek clarification on confusing issues or questions. It is true that interviewer bias can affect telephone interview results, but a carefully designed questionnaire can effectively limit this impact.

A primary advantage of telephone interviews is their limited time requirement. The number of telephone interviews completed on an hourly basis by far exceeds that possible in personal or mail interviewing — typically, between three and ten interviews can be completed per hour.

It is relatively easy to hire and train staff to conduct phone interviews. The number of interviewers can be quickly expanded to speed the interview process, overcoming the majority of time constraints.

Further, telephone response rates are generally greater than for mail surveys because call-backs are easily made. As a result, telephone interviews are used extensively in conjunction with secondary research to expand, clarify, and confirm secondary findings and to identify trends and issues as they occur.

Figure 3-4
Mail Survey Cost Estimation*

	Equipment Costs	Labor Costs	Fees	Total
Mailing List				
In-house development	$ _____	$ _____	$ _____	$ _____
Rental	$ _____	$ _____	$ _____	$ _____
Questionnaire Preparation/ Design	$ _____	$ _____	$ _____	$ _____
Mailing Costs	$ _____	$ _____	$ _____	$ _____
Stationery Envelopes, and Printing Fees	$ _____	$ _____	$ _____	$ _____
Statistical Analysis Design	$ _____	$ _____	$ _____	$ _____
Telephone Follow-Up	$ _____	$ _____	$ _____	$ _____
Data Processing and Analysis	$ _____	$ _____	$ _____	$ _____
TOTALS	$ _____	$ _____	$ _____	$ _____

* (Assume 10,000 pieces of mail)

The main advantages of telephone interviewing are its:

- Cost-effectiveness compared to personal interviews;
- Virtually unlimited geographical potential;
- Call-backs can be used to reach difficult-to-find respondents;
- Time per interview that can be easily controlled; and
- Large numbers of respondents that can be interviewed in a comparatively short time period.

Telephone Interview Disadvantages. Telephone interviews to obtain primary data have certain drawbacks.

Drawbacks of telephone interviews include:

- Cost escalation if large geographic areas are involved;
- Lack of visual aids, which can be difficult;
- Lack of face-to-face contact with the respondent;
- Interviews that can be easily terminated by the respondent; and
- Possible bias that may be caused by interviewer style.

Generally, these disadvantages may be overcome by careful questionnaire design and interviewer persistence. Note that cost factors are still small when compared to the potential costs of personal and mail survey methods.

Telephone Interview Considerations. Relevant costs for each stage of the telephone interviewing process can be determined by breaking down each stage into a series of steps. To begin the telephone research process, you need to:

- Determine study objectives;
- Determine and locate appropriate lists of contacts;
- Formulate the questionnaire;
- Sample ten interviews to determine questionnaire efficiency (a testing process);
- Revise questionnaire, if appropriate;
- Conduct interviews;
- Transcribe interviews; and
- Process data.

Several factors affect the costs of determining and locating necessary contacts, such as whether the contact list is acquired from outside sources or formulated in-house. Trade association charges for relevant lists vary but generally range from $300 to $550 per list of 2,000 names. Costs are further increased if lists are sorted.

Bimonthly publications and directories, such as the Standard Rate and Data Service (SRDS) and the Medical Device Register, can provide an idea of list sources by area of specialty. Other sources of information on where to acquire lists include trade magazines, publication houses, and list houses such as Edith Roman.

Costs of assembling the list in-house can vary widely. General cost considerations can include trade directory and index acquisition costs, as well as, labor and equipment costs of compiling suitable lists.

Costs will vary depending on the:

- Type of interview sample (Do you wish to contact CEOs or market managers?);

- Types of questions you wish answered;

- Geographical scope of the survey;

- Requirements for quality of interviewers (Is some level of expertise required?); and

- Telephone charges per interview.

Figure 3-5 provides a worksheet to consider costs when estimating telephone survey costs.

After estimating the costs of these individual factors, total the costs to arrive at a cost per interview estimate. To estimate total cost of the telephone interviewing phase, multiply the cost per interview by the number of interviews to be conducted and add this to the cost of list acquisition or development and data processing.

Personal interviews are the oldest method of obtaining primary data and remain a widely-used method of market research. During personal interviews, the interviewer directs questions to the respondent or respondents face-to-face. The interviewer generally follows a set line of questioning from memory.

Survey Option 3 – The Personal Interview

Personal Interview Advantages. Personal interviews are more flexible than telephone or mail survey alternatives and can be effectively used to administer any type of questionnaire. Personal interviews allow the respondent to use visual aids to clarify questions and to request further explanation of questions that may not be clear.

Personal interviews can run longer than either mail or telephone surveys, thus providing more information. The main advantages of the personal interview in primary data gathering are:

- Greater interviewer control;

- Suitable for collection of highly detailed data;

- Increased respondent cooperation;

- Highly useful for vital interviews with key respondents; and

- Useful for discussions of complex products and concepts.

Personal Interview Disadvantages. The main disadvantage of personal interviews is the time involved. Total personal interview time can be substantial because interviewers must travel to and from interviews and organize appointments. The number of interviewers may be increased to reduce the total time requirements, but this can be undesirable because of the costs associated with training and coordinating additional staff.

The potential for interviewer bias affecting the interview is greatest during the personal interview. The interviewer is more of a force during the personal interview and can often impress his or her opinions on the respondent. Major drawbacks of the personal interview are:

Figure 3-5
Worksheet to Estimate Telephone Survey Costs

1. **Contact List**
   List acquisition costs
      Cost per number of names _____
      Additional sorting costs _____
      Labor costs _____
         Total $_____

   List development costs
      Cost per number of names _____
      Cost of trade directory acquisition _____
      Additional source costs _____
      Labor and equipment costs _____
         Total $_____

2. **Questionnaire Formulation**
   Staff costs _____
   Resource costs _____
   Equipment costs _____
      Total $_____

3. **Questionnaire Check**
   Staff costs _____
   Telephone charges _____
      Total $_____

4. **Questionnaire Revision (where necessary)**
   Staff costs _____
   Resource costs _____
   Equipment costs _____
      Total $_____

5. **Interview Process (costs per interview)**
   Telephone charges per interview _____
   Staff costs _____
      x   Total number of interviews
         Total $_____

6. **Preparation of Interview Reports**
   Staff costs _____
   Equipment costs _____
      Total $_____

Total Costs $_____

- The process is more costly and time consuming than available alternatives, particularly when travel is required;

- Interviewers must be well-trained and qualified;

- Interviewer bias can distort results;

- Significant planning is required if you want to avoid high costs; and

- Extensive procedures are required to ensure potential respondents are adequately qualified.

Personal Interview Cost Considerations. Personal interviewing is generally accepted as the most expensive survey method for primary data gathering. Depending on the geographical scope of the survey, personal interviewing is often ill-advised despite its effectiveness in information acquisition.

Practically all market research has two things in common: it is generally heavily time-constrained and costs of the research process must usually be closely monitored. The personal interview method includes both these constraints, as any personal interview program is generally both expensive and time consuming.

The primary costs of the personal interviewing process are:

- Contact list development or acquisition costs;

- Initial phone contact costs (to arrange interviews);

- Questionnaire development costs;

- Travel costs;

- Labor costs; and

- Interview processing costs.

The worksheet in Figure 3-6 provides guidelines for calculating costs of any interview.

When setting up personal interviews, select the most appropriate interview category to receive the optimum response for your project. Market research interviews are generally classified into two categories — structure and directness.

Select the Right Interview Categories for Your Project

Structured Interviews. Structure refers to the degree an interviewer is obliged to precisely follow the wording and instructions of the interview questionnaire.

Successful structured interviews must be accurate. A significant degree of knowledge of the topic is important when the questionnaire is designed.

Interviewers can alter the course of an interview by adding or deleting questions, altering question sequence, probing deeper into certain questions, and changing the emphasis of questions. Structured interviews minimize the potential for this to occur.

Structured interviews do offer a significant number of advantages. The major advantages of structured interviews are that the:

Figure 3-6
Worksheet to Determine Personal Interview Program Costs

1. Contact List Costs
    List development costs
        Cost per number of names   _____
        Additional sorting costs   _____
        Labor costs   _____
            Total $_____

    List development costs
        Cost of trade directory acquisition   _____
        Additional source costs   _____
        Labor and equipment costs   _____
            Total $_____

2. Initial Phone Contact Costs (to arrange interviews)
    Labor costs $_____
    Telephone charges   _____
            Total $_____

3. Questionnaire Formulation Costs
    Labor costs $_____
    Resource costs   _____
            Total $_____

4. Travel Costs
    Transportation $_____
    Accommodations (if necessary) $_____
    General expenses $_____
            Total $_____

5. Interview Costs
    Labor costs $_____
        x   Total number of interviews
            Total $_____

6. Interview Processing Costs and the Preparation of Interview Reports
    Labor costs   _____
    Equipment costs   _____
            Total $_____

Total Costs $_____

- Effects of interviewer bias tend to be minimized when interview questionnaires are highly structured;

- Project costs can be cut by using less skilled or less qualified interviewers to read questions and record responses; and

- Interviews are easily applied to statistical and quantitative analysis.

Unstructured Interviews. Unstructured interviews are useful in market research projects where knowledge of the variables being examined is significant, and for exploring new technologies or markets. The primary advantage of unstructured interviews is that skilled interviewers can usually elicit detailed and complete information when allowed a loose format questionnaire. This type of interview is useful when interviewing industry experts and technologists.

Direct Interviews. Direct interviews involve asking the respondent questions that will make the underlying objectives of the survey apparent. The majority of market research questionnaires are direct, making the focus of interest obvious to the respondent.

Direct interviews offer certain advantages. Questions asked directly are usually simple to understand and result in easily interpreted responses.

Indirect Interviews. Indirect interviews do not reveal the objective of the research. This type of interview is basically used only when direct interviewing methods are not applicable. The difficulty of creating indirect interview questionnaires and interpreting the responses often discourages use of this method. Indirect interviews can be advantageous if respondents are unwilling to answer direct questions on sensitive topics.

If you have selected the mail survey method, you will want to follow some basic guidelines to get started.

How to Set Up and Conduct Mail Surveys

Construct or Acquire a Comprehensive Mailing List. Construct or acquire a comprehensive mailing list. A mailing list is essential to the success of your mail survey. Therefore, one of the first tasks should be assembling a comprehensive list of contacts, keeping in mind the following factors:

- Approximately 100 responses are required for statistical analysis. Remember, typical response rates vary between 1 and 4 percent without response encouragement and from 4 to 20 percent when response is encouraged. Design the size of the list with this consideration in mind. The list must be large enough to provide a statistically significant sample.

- Contacts should be individuals with some degree of expertise in the area being researched.

- The list should be homogeneous to as great an extent as possible.

Determine the Sample Size. The sample size required will depend on the:

- Quantity to estimate (Note: the more you know about distribution of this quantity in the total population, the lower the sample size required); and

- Degree of confidence required in the results.

Construct a Questionnaire. Questionnaire design used in a mail survey should be your primary consideration. Vital points to consider during mail survey questionnaire design are listed below.

- Determine goals and objectives of the research project.

- Include only questions requiring answers that will make a difference in planning or decision making and are relevant to the project objectives.

- Keep the questionnaire as brief as possible. If the survey will not fit on one or two pages, use an 11x17 piece of paper. The fewer the pages, the greater the response — five pages should be the maximum mail survey length.

- Make sure the questionnaire is easy to read.

- Make questions easy to answer. Use closed end multiple choice or a yes-no checking structure whenever possible.

- Be sure to ask questions clearly.

- Reassure respondents as to their anonymity (if possible).

- Make sure questions are worded so they do not encourage specific desired answers.

- Thoroughly test the questionnaire. This is extremely important for response rate and answer quality.

- Design questions so they are adaptable for computer processing.

Design a Cover Letter. A cover letter encourages greater response rates. Make sure the cover letter looks professional — avoid a junk mail appearance. Important points to consider during design of the mail survey cover letter are listed below.

- Let potential respondents know exactly who you are.

- Describe in detail the survey and its goals.

- Ensure the confidentiality of responses (if possible).

- Explain how the survey may assist the respondent as well as yourself.

- Encourage a prompt response.

- Reassure potential respondents that a salesperson will not contact them.

Consider Ways to Encourage Response. Offering the potential respondent some form of reward for compliance encourages response. Perhaps you might stress the opportunities for information sharing that you may offer if the survey is completed. If response rates are initially disappointing, use follow-up calls or letters as a means of encouraging increased response. Here are some other helpful tips to encourage response.

- Before mailing, test the questionnaire in several telephone interviews to ensure there are no ambiguities.

- Provide a self-addressed, stamped envelope in the mailing.

- Several good microcomputer-based survey/statistical analysis software packages exist. Use of one of these packages is generally necessary for all but the most basic tabulation analysis.

- Use a third party, such as an independent market research company, to encourage a better response rate and superior information. Potential respondents are typically suspicious if asked to participate in a survey organized by their market competitors.

Assume that you have developed or acquired a list of contacts. The following steps will assist you in a successful telephone research process.

How to Set Up and Conduct Telephone Surveys

Use a Well-designed Questionnaire. Once you have designed a questionnaire, test it on 15 respondents and assess its efficiency. If the questionnaire is inadequate, carefully revise it to ensure flexibility and clarity.

Be Professional. Your introduction is one of the most vital points in the telephone interview. An example of a cold-call interview — where the respondent was not prepared in advance — is provided in Figure 3-7.

**Figure 3-7
Cold-Call Telephone Interview**

"Hello, Ms. Fields. My name is Mark Stevens. I am a research analyst with _____. We are a company specializing in _____. I am currently conducting research into the area of_____. I understand that your company is a major competitor in this area and I would like to ask you a few questions regarding _____."

Be Upfront and Persistent. Inform the respondent exactly how you selected his or her name. Do not expect objections or mention proprietary information concerns, interview length, or confidentiality aspects unless the respondent asks. If the respondent expresses concern, provide reassurance. If you are unable to reach the contact on your first attempt, note it on your contact sheet and call back later.

Include the questions provided in Figure 3-8 in your telephone interview if you are seeking competitive market or product information.

Figure 3-8
Telephone Interview Market and Technical Questions

- Could you tell me a little about your product?
- What is the product price?
- When was the product introduced into the market?
- Is the product well-accepted in the marketplace?
- How many units are in service today?
- Who is currently using the product?
- Who are your major competitors?
- How many people does your firm employ?
- What is your annual turnover?
- What is the trend in sales?
- What technical trends are foreseen?
- How is your product differentiated in the market?
- How is the market divided between manufacturers?
- What type of market growth is occurring?
- Who else should I talk to?
- What else would you like to see in a study such as this?

Establish a Positive Rapport. The quality of information derived from a telephone or personal interview depends on the quality of the relationship established between the interviewer and the respondent. Interviews are most effective when the interviewer exhibits subtle, sensitive combinations of patience, tact, active listening, empathy, persistence, and a willingness to learn.

The essence of telephone and personal interviewing lies in genuinely eliciting the interest of the respondent. The interviewer must transcend his or her immediate concerns for deadlines and quick data gathering and focus on establishing a positive relationship with the respondent.

Listen Carefully. Active listening is a critical technique for demonstrating an understanding of what the respondent is really saying and facilitating his or her continued exploration of the marketplace. By communicating a genuine respect for the respondent's concerns and responsibilities, you create an atmosphere conducive to mutually examining the salient features of the contemporary market. An advantage of the telephone interview is the potential to trade information because it provides an incentive to the respondent to participate.

How to Set Up and Conduct Personal Surveys

Personal interviews are extremely effective when extensive discussions of complicated product technology concepts are required. Do not conduct a personal interview when a telephone interview would be just as effective.

Use the same process of establishing a contact list that was discussed in detail earlier in this chapter.

Make a Good First Impression. Arranging the personal interview. Contact the potential respondent by phone and request an appointment. This initial phone contact is the key to a successful personal interview. Follow these key points during the initial telephone contact.

- Be confident — Uncertainty discourages cooperation. Indicate advantages of the interview to the respondent as well as to yourself. Stress the opportunity to share industry gossip.

- Don't hedge — Get to the point of your call quickly and keep the discussion professional.

- Assure the respondent that the interview will be as brief as possible.

- Suggest an interview time and offer the potential respondent reasons why it should not be delayed.

- Indicate how you were referred to the respondent. Flatter his or her stature in the industry.

- If the respondent hesitates, assure that he or she will not be quoted, his or her name will be kept anonymous, and you will not attempt to uncover proprietary data.

- If the potential respondent is unavailable at the time you would like to meet, request another time.

Make a Lasting Impression. After the respondent has agreed to the interview, the rest is comparatively simple. How you conduct yourself is the key to a rewarding interview. The tips listed below demonstrate how to conduct a successful personal interview.

- Never be late — Tardiness is inexcusable. Arrive early to give yourself adequate time to locate the respondent.

- Maintain professional formality when initially meeting the respondent. Allow the interviewee to set the tone for the meeting. If he or she becomes informal follow suit — otherwise, remain formal.

- Briefly discuss the reasons for the meeting. Remind the respondent of your goals and objectives to avoid any ambiguity during the course of discussion.

- Memorize the questionnaire prior to the interview to avoid constant referral to your notes.

- Watch the respondent carefully for any visual cues he or she might give during the discussion.

- If the meaning of certain responses is unclear, request clarification.

- Remember to take notes, but don't start immediately. Allow the conversation to flow smoothly before removing your note pad.

- At the conclusion of the interview, politely thank the respondent and ask if you can get back to him or her to clear up any ambiguous issues that might arise.

- When the personal interview is complete, review your notes and immediately write a detailed transcript while the points are fresh in your mind. If gray areas arise, call the respondent and try to clarify them or arrange a short interview to avoid misconceptions.

Effective Mail Survey Examples

Figures 3-9 and 3-10 are good examples for designing a mail survey cover letter and questionnaire.

Figure 3-9
Example of a Mail Survey Cover Letter
Hewlett-Packard Computer Software Survey

Dear HP Computer User:

Market Intelligence Research Company, an international market research firm, is conducting a research study in the area of HP Computer Data Center Management (DCM) software. Data Center Management software performs functions such as:

    System Access Control and Security
    Batch Job management
    Tape Library Management
    Terminal Network Management
    Resource/Data Center Cost Allocation

As part of this study, we are conducting surveys of HP Computer DP managers as well as of DCM software vendors.

The purpose of this study is to enable HP computer software vendors to better understand and serve the computing needs of HP Computer users. Your response is essential to obtain valid information that will allow the software industry to adequately address the data center management problems of HP users. Simply fill out the survey (10 minutes) and drop it in the postage-paid envelope we've provided.

Your individual responses will be maintained in strict confidence and will only be aggregated with other responses. No salesperson will call as a result of this survey.

In appreciation of your time and comments, we would like to provide you with a free copy of our results, which may be obtained by entering your name and address on the survey. I would appreciate receiving your response by Friday, August 29.

Thank you for your time. If you have any questions, I may be reached at (815) 955-3340.

Sincerely,

Chris Nugent
Project Director

Figure 3-10
Example of a Mail Survey Questionnaire Design

<u>**Hewlett-Packard Computer Software Survey**</u>

Your Organization: _____

1. Please indicate your organization's industry area:
    ❑ Manufacturing   ❑ Business Services
    ❑ Banking/Finance   ❑ Government
    ❑ Electronics   ❑ Distribution
    ❑ Other:_____

2. Indicate the approximate size of your organization:
    ❑ Less than $5 million   ❑ $51-100 million
    ❑ $6-10 million   ❑ $101 million - $1 billion
    ❑ $11-50 million   ❑ Greater than $1 billion

Your Computer System: _____

3. Does your plant or site have an HP computer system?
    ❑ Yes   ❑ No

    Indicate the number of HP computer systems at your site: _____

    Total number of HP computers in your company: _____

4. Indicate the size distribution of the HP Computer system(s) at your site:
    ❑ Large (Series 6X, 7X)   Number installed _____
    ❑ Medium (Series 44, 48, 5X)   Number installed _____
    ❑ Small (Series 3X, 40, 42)   Number installed _____

5. Are the HP systems at your site used in a distributed processing
    environment?   ❑ Yes   ❑ No

    If yes, how many CPUs are in the network? _____

6. How many terminals are installed at your location? _____

7. How many operations shifts are staffed at your site?
    ❑ One   ❑ Two   ❑ Three

    Days per week of data center operation: _____

Figure 3-10 (continued)

8. Please indicate the source (OCS, Tymlabs, Computing Capabilities, Carolian Systems, Design/3000, in-house, or other) of your HP data center management software: _____

In the far right column, indicate by circling your level of satisfaction (3=high, 2=medium, 1=low) with the software:

Function Module	Name of Vendor or Package	Satisfaction Level		
Batch Job Management	_____	3	2	1
Access Control and Security	_____	3	2	1
Tape Library Management	_____	3	2	1
Data Center Cost Allocation	_____	3	2	1
Terminal Network Monitoring	_____	3	2	1
Other:_____	_____	3	2	1

9. Rate the relative importance of the following functions to the management of your DP center:

	More Important			Less Important	
Batch Job Management	5	4	3	2	1
Access Control and Security	5	4	3	2	1
Tape Library Management	5	4	3	2	1
Data Center Cost Allocation	5	4	3	2	1
Terminal Network Monitoring	5	4	3	2	1
Central Console for Multiple CPUs	5	4	3	2	1
Spool Management	5	4	3	2	1
Program Library Management	5	4	3	2	1
System Backup (Utilities)	5	4	3	2	1
System Performance Monitoring	5	4	3	2	1
Other: _____	5	4	3	2	1

10. Please indicate which applications software you are using (check all that apply):
    ❑ ASK Manman   ❑ SFD/3000   ❑ Collier-Jackson
    ❑ HP MM/PM   ❑ MCBA   ❑ Other:_____

Figure 3-10 (continued)

11. Please rate the relative importance of the following factors in your DECISION TO ACQUIRE data center management software. Circle numbers, on a scale of:

5=Very Important   3=Moderately Important   1=Not Important

	Very Important			Not Important	
Ease of Use	5	4	3	2	1
Reputation of Vendor	5	4	3	2	1
Trade Journal Advertising	5	4	3	2	1
Trade Journal Editorial	5	4	3	2	1
Recommendation of					
Hardware Vendor	5	4	3	2	1
User Recommendation	5	4	3	2	1
Price	5	4	3	2	1
Vendor Trade					
Show Attendance	5	4	3	2	1
Functionality/Features	5	4	3	2	1
Customer Training/Education	5	4	3	2	1
Vendor Support	5	4	3	2	1
Networking Ability	5	4	3	2	1
Reliability	5	4	3	2	1
Ease of Implementation	5	4	3	2	1
Documentation	5	4	3	2	1
Other:_____	5	4	3	2	1

12. Do you agree or disagree with the following statements about YOUR MOST IMPORTANT DATA CENTER MANAGEMENT SOFTWARE? Write in the name of your most important data center management software package:

_____

_____

	Agree Strongly			Disagree Strongly	
Software is easy to use	5	4	3	2	1
Price of software is reasonable	5	4	3	2	1
Support of vendor is effective	5	4	3	2	1
Reputation of vendor is favorable	5	4	3	2	1
Functionality/features adequate	5	4	3	2	1
Networking ability is adequate	5	4	3	2	1
Software is reliable	5	4	3	2	1
Sufficient training/education	5	4	3	2	1
Software is easy to implement	5	4	3	2	1
Documentation is adequate	5	4	3	2	1
Other: _____	5	4	3	2	1

Figure 3-10 (continued)

13. Please indicate which computer system(s), if any, you plan to acquire in the next twelve months:

Number of Systems

❏ HP Spectrum   _____
❏ HP (Series #_____)   _____
❏ Other: (Mfg. _____)   _____

14. indicate which data center management/automation software you plan to acquire in the next twelve months (check all that apply):

Function   Vendor or Package

❏ Access Control and Security   _____
❏ Batch Job Management   _____
❏ Tape Library Management   _____
❏ Data Center Cost Allocation   _____
❏ Terminal Network Monitoring   _____
❏ Other: _____   _____

15. Which data center management/automation companies and products are you aware of (check all that apply):

Companies

❏ Carolian Systems Co.   ❏ Chestnut Data Sys.
❏ Computing Capabilities (CCC) ❏ Design/3000
❏ Operations Control Sys. (OCS) ❏ Tymlabs Corp.
❏ Vesoft

Packages

❏ JMS/3000   ❏ DCA   ❏ MAESTRO
❏ TMS   ❏ TAPES   ❏ CDS/Acorn
❏ RADAR   ❏ Security/3000 ❏ Sysview
❏ OCS/3000   ❏ UNISPOOL   ❏ OCS/Network

16. What operations problems are you having with your HP computer data center?

_____
_____

Thank you for your time. If you would like a FREE summary of the results of this study, please complete the following:

NAME: _____ TITLE: _____

ORGANIZATION: _____

STREET: _____

CITY: _____ STATE: _____ ZIP: _____

Please return the survey in the postage-paid envelope by Friday, August 29. Thank you for your time and comments.

Similar questionnaires may be used for both telephone and personal interviews. Figure 3-11 illustrates a questionnaire successfully used in an actual, combined personal/telephone interview program. Responses to the majority of questions were obtained in all interviews.

Figure 3-11
Personal/Telephone Interview Questionnaire Design

Designed for interviews with marketing and sales VPs, product, sales, and market managers at companies producing defibrillator (heart-saving) monitors for medical applications.

Interviewer: _____

Date: _____

Time: _____

Respondent Name: _____

Title: _____

Company: _____

Phone: _____

1. Could you tell me a little about your product?

2. Where are the units most frequently used?

3. What are your feelings about the recent debate regarding high output versus low output defibrillators?

4. Is there any trend to the creation of an industry standard defibrillator monitor waveform?

5. What product features are most favored by end-users?

6. Is the coronary care unit or the mobile application market the largest market segment for this product?

7. Have recently enacted government reimbursement regulations impacted this market?

8. What forces are currently driving market growth?

9. What is the average rate of replacement on a defibrillator monitor?

10. What is the average product price?

11. Has the market experienced much growth in the last decade? Please estimate annual percentage growth rate of dollar sales.

Figure 3-11 (continued)

12. Could you give me your estimate, in units and dollars, of last year's size of the U.S. market for this product?

13. What annual growth rate do you anticipate for the market through the year 2000?

14. What was the approximate value of U.S. exports of this product last year?

15. What was the value of your sales of this product last year?

16. What are the major market sub-segments for this product?

17. Do you anticipate any new technical trends in the market? Would you identify them?

18. Who are your major market competitors?

19. Could you rank the main competitors in this market and their relative shares of the market?

20. Can you suggest any sources of published data that provide historical production data on this product?

21. Are there any other issues that you feel should be addressed?

Selection Criteria for the Survey Method

No single method of primary data gathering is suitable for all situations. The particular information requirements of the project, the type of information that can be derived via each method, and time and budget constraints should determine method selection.

To acquire the information needed at the lowest cost, analyze all available options to determine which methods meet your needs. Figure 3-12 outlines strengths and weaknesses of the various available methods.

Survey Research Conclusions

Despite the difficulties associated with survey research, it is the main method of primary data gathering in market research. Gathering information in this way remains, despite its problems, the most efficient way to contact a diverse group of respondents. Accurate, timely, primary data acquisition is crucial to the completion of market research analysis. Thus, the importance of developing accurate techniques for survey interview completion and analysis cannot be overstated.

Figure 3-12
Selection Criteria for Available Survey Methods

Selection Criteria	Telephone	Personal	Mail
1. Cost	Good	Bad	Good
2. Probable response	Fair	Fair	Fair
3. Time	Excellent	Poor	Poor
4. Interviewer bias	Fair	Poor	Excellent
5. Accuracy on proprietary questions	Fair	Fair	Good
6. Capacity for confidential data collection	Good	Good	Fair
7. Adaptability for complex questionnaires	Good	Good	Poor
8. Level of sample control	Good	Good	Fair
9. Ability to secure a large sample	Good	Poor	Excellent

Notes

Chapter 4

The Value of Trade Shows

Using trade shows as a source of market information during the research process can save both time and money. Trade shows represent an ideal place to conduct preliminary research; a multitude of existing end-users, prospective end-users, and competitors are conveniently located under one roof for a certain period of time.

The trade show gives industry participants a unique opportunity to gain a superior understanding of end-user needs, competitor strategies, and general technological and market trends.

Types of Research Data Available at Trade Shows

Several types of research data are available at trade shows. Major types of information available at trade shows are:

- Marketing strategies;

- Product information;

- Competitor information;

- Customer interest levels/end-user perceptions; and

- Technical trends.

Identify New Marketing Strategies

Trade shows can be valuable for businesses developing a new marketing strategy or enhancing and improving an existing strategy.

The trade show presents an opportunity to obtain a better understanding of the thought patterns, needs, and requirements of existing and potential end-users. Potential unexploited market niches can be effectively identified during trade show research. Is your product lacking features that would enhance its ability to sell? Trade shows also offer you an opportunity to determine features that can improve the marketability of a certain product.

In attempting to determine optimal markets for targeting your product or estimating how salable it is, you have the opportunity to discuss the marketplace with both retailers and distributors. You can gain an insight into positive and negative perceptions regarding the product and the company and modify marketing strategies accordingly.

Market strategy development data available at trade shows can be separated effectively into nine distinct categories. Figure 4-1 illustrates these categories, the flow of trade show data, and the type of data available at trade shows most likely to be used for market strategy development. Once the data has been successfully assembled and analyzed the data, you can effectively review existing market strategy, identify its strengths and weaknesses and suggest appropriate modifications.

Develop Critical Product Strategies

A trade show is an excellent place to acquire feedback on new and existing products. Increasing numbers of companies are timing their new product releases for announcements at trade shows, linking their market research to product introduction.

By asking well-planned questions of end-users and potential end-users attending the trade show, you can acquire vital information regarding the acceptance of newly implemented features and factors they may have overlooked. The types of questions directed to end-users and potential end-users will vary depending on the nature of the product, such as whether it is a totally new model or an improvement on an existing device.

Seminars held at trade shows can provide you with a wealth of information concerning future product development trends. Leading industry experts will often speak at trade show seminars. If the speaker is aware of potential technological developments, interesting information on future product trends can often be acquired. Seminars also provide an opportunity to share opinions and exchange information with other industry experts.

Many researchers emphasize trade show research during product development to discover design problems before market introduction. Larger companies often send product planning and marketing representatives to trade shows while their product is being developed so researchers can assess predominantly demanded product features and capabilities and the direction of competitor development. These features can then be integrated into the product design.

Gather Key Competitor Information

The trade show is a vital source of competitor information and often represents the only chance to gain free access to the competitions' products for comparison and evaluation. Competitors often reveal a great deal about new products and strategies during trade shows despite their attempts during the year to conceal the thrust of their marketing strategies.

Trade shows provide an opportunity to talk with competitor salespeople (who are often extremely free with information) and examine competitor product literature. The trade show can be one of the most suitable places to gain a rapid, fairly accurate idea of the extent of a competitor's marketing effort, dynamics, and growth prospects.

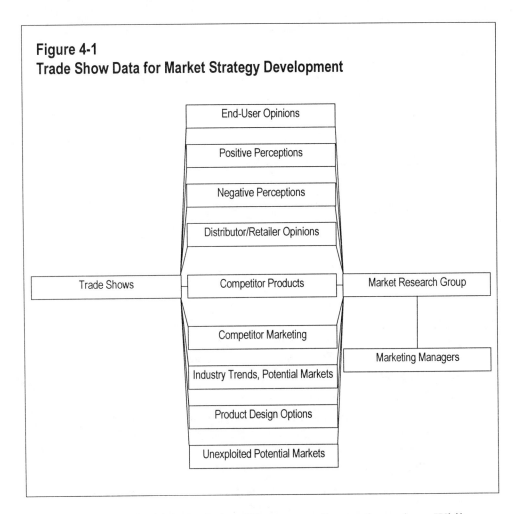

Figure 4-1
Trade Show Data for Market Strategy Development

Companies diverge widely in their willingness to discuss themselves. While some companies are very open, others are not open. For example, Japanese companies are known for their willingness to disclose their intended production schedules, while U.S. and European companies are typically more discreet about divulging information. However, do not become discouraged — a diligent researcher can often acquire a general impression of sales magnitude during product discussion.

Most industries feel that all displays are intended for public viewing. So the trade show provides an ideal environment for closely examining competitor products. You can gain valuable information on your competition at trade shows, including:

- Competitor market strategies;
- Competitor product information;
- Competitor dynamics; and
- Competitor production and sales data.

How to Conduct Trade Show Research

Deciding the groups on which to focus will vary with the requirements and objectives of the research project. If you want to determine how successful a particular product is in the marketplace, the focus should be on end-user research. If the research problem revolves around the sales potential of a particular product, the research effort should focus on distributors or retailers.

Several key groups provide valuable information for the trade show researcher, including:

- End-users and potential end-users,
- Competitors,
- Distributors,
- Industry experts, and
- Press groups.

End-users and Potential End-users

End-users and potential end-users can provide the researcher with an excellent idea of how a product line and company are perceived in the marketplace. Trade shows provide you a chance to talk to end-users who may have positive or negative perceptions about the product and the company. This type of data can be vital in enhancing product design and market strategy. The following steps detail how to talk to end users.

- Be receptive — Attempt to get as many in-depth comments and insights as you can. Have the end-user explain problems he or she has had with the product or the company. Have end-users with positive perceptions list what they consider the strong points about your company and product offering.

- Take notes — During your discussions with end-users, document each interview to develop a solid analysis.

- Be methodical — Make sure you interview enough people for a representative sample. Record the name, position, and background of each respondent. This is important and may help you convince company management of the value of your findings.

Competitors

Trade shows often offer you an opportunity to discuss specific issues with the competition. While certain competitors are extremely protective during discussions with other industry participants, the majority appear to take the healthy attitude that the trade show is a venue for information exchange and the dissemination of ideas. Use the following steps when talking to competitors.

- Be honest — Resorting to false name badges when entering a competitor's booth is not advisable.

- Be persistent — Occasionally you will be dismissed with a promotional brochure. In situations like this, reciprocity is the best tactic. Arrange for a mutual tour of each other's exhibits and the chance to engage in detailed information sharing. When visiting the competitor's booth, take rough notes and listen to the comments of booth staff. If booth noise is distracting, arrange to meet a member of the competitor staff away from the exhibit.

Salespeople will often discuss a great deal more than the product they are offering. Booth personnel are typically willing to provide useful information such as company size and strategy. Although these personnel are limited in the data they possess, they can provide a helpful picture of a particular competitor.

Distributors

Distributors can provide a fairly accurate picture of typical end-user product preferences in certain geographic regions. Distributor research can also prove invaluable during product development, providing data on desirable product packaging or current end-user demands for particular product features.

Industry Experts

The quality of speakers and topics included in a trade show seminar program are principal reasons for executives of leading U.S. companies to attend trade shows. The educational aspect of trade show seminars is usually a significant drawing card for the researcher. The information imparted by expert speakers, particularly if the speaker focuses on the latest technical and market trends in the industry, can prove invaluable.

Recent surveys indicate that vice president directors, managers of information systems, office systems managers, and other upper and middle management will generally attend key trade show seminars, presenting a researcher with the ideal venue to discuss trends with high-level experts.

When talking to experts, wait until the educational seminar is complete before approaching other attendees. Target potentially valuable sources of information before the seminar. Take notes on the trends and projections outlined in the seminar and ask other experts attending for their opinions. In this manner, you can develop an exceedingly accurate picture of product development trends, competitive trends, market growth, and other valuable information.

To encourage conversation, offer your opinions on the information divulged during the seminar. Remain broad-minded and open to a wide variety of opinions. If possible, take notes on the comments of attending experts for subsequent analysis.

Press Groups

A valuable information resource at trade shows is the large number of press people who regularly attend the shows. Members of the press are not affiliated with any company and can acquire large quantities of information that would not have been divulged to competitors.

Representatives of the press attending trade shows are fairly easy to approach and involve in discussions regarding industry trends. The following steps enumerate the ideal method for obtaining information from the press.

- Discuss show and seminar highlights with several press people — Carefully note the separate opinions of each. After cultivating a number of conversations with members of the trade show press, examine the notes you have taken during your discussions. Look for points of consensus and disagreement and attempt to develop an overview of industry trends.

- Gather inside information — Members of the press can provide an insight into the so-called backroom products of your competitors. Certain products are often shown only to prospective end-users and members of press groups. By close association with trade show press representatives, you can gain insight into products you may not otherwise have known about or been shown.

The Role of Planning in Trade Show Research

Planning is essential to effectively use the trade show as a source of market research information. As a researcher, you must be aware of exactly what information you need to acquire.

Although the overwhelming majority of U.S. companies conduct some form of market intelligence gathering at trade shows, their research is often poorly planned and executed. The typical trade show attendee, having received the trip to the show as a type of reward, may wander about aimlessly without clear objectives. A detailed plan will help overcome this problem.

Japanese companies have long recognized the value of the trade show as a research tool. Larger Japanese companies often have entire staffs whose sole job is to attend and report on trade shows. The advantage of this strategy is that it often takes a regular, experienced trade show attendee to recognize real developments and potential future trends.

As a researcher, it is vital to have a floor plan of the exhibits and a list of manufacturers attending the trade show. This enables selection of potential interview respondents to maximize the cohesiveness of the research effort and ensures methodical coverage of all exhibits. The following considerations can assist in better planning and organizing the trade show research effort.

Plan Your Staff

Choosing the appropriate trade show research team or researcher is a key factor in planning a successful trade show research effort. Often, everyone at the show will want to do their own thing — each product manager wants to personally examine every product. This is fine if the company is large enough to afford the time and effort involved. But most companies should assign research team members to well-defined tasks relating to their area of expertise.

The size of the trade show can also provide an important consideration. Small shows can generally be covered by one or two people.

Maintain a Team Focus and Direction

It is essential to calculate and outline the desired focus and depth of the research during the planning stage of trade show research. This avoids subsequent inconsistencies in the scope of research among your research team members.

The focus of the trade show research program should never be too narrow. A significant challenge confronting the research team is to maintain a broad perspective — don't focus on your own particular product type. Tomorrow's competing product may come from a segment of the industry you never expected. A wider focus enables you to better anticipate potential competition and the direction of the market. You may discover insights you had previously not even considered.

Planning the Trade Show Report

If the trade show data is not destined to become part of a larger report, assign a single member of the trade show research team to prepare a summary report about the show. The individual preparing the report should use input from each member of the research team.

It is essential that each member of the research team take accurate and detailed notes while attending the trade show. These notes should then be turned over to the person abstracting the trade show data to keep the report consistent and easy to read.

A camera, if permitted at the show, is an ideal means of documentation.

End-user Perceptions and Surveys

End-user and prospective end-user perceptions of both new and existing products can be a vital research tool. The trade show is an excellent location for end-user research since many customers and prospective customers are conveniently located under one roof.

Surveys are one of the most effective ways to get an impression or cross-section of end-user opinion. The three following methods are currently advocated as the most effective means of conducting end-user surveys at trade shows:

- Written surveys,

- Focus groups, and

- Verbal and written interviews.

Written Surveys

Questionnaires can be effective at trade shows and provide the added advantage of immediate feedback. Feedback from mail surveys may take weeks to appear. The trade show provides you the opportunity to hand out questionnaires and obtain immediate results.

Written surveys can be given to end-users and potential end-users as they enter your company's booth. It is comparatively simple for you to modify the questionnaire as incoming results give an improved indication of end-user opinion. On the first day of the show, if your questionnaire survey indicates your primary marketing platform should be to offer a fully-featured product, begin pushing the product as fully-featured on day two of the show and observe any changes in questionnaire response.

Carefully structure the questions to avoid ambiguity. Try to get end-user feedback about product performance, impressions of your company, and so forth. Your research goal will dictate your questionnaire format. The key is to make the questionnaire simple so you do not discourage busy trade show attendees from completing one. When designing a trade show questionnaire:

- Keep questionnaires brief;

- Depending on research project goals, set an informal or formal style; and

- Structure questionnaires so they are detailed enough to provide the desired answers.

If you are going to attempt a trade show survey, keep it short and simple.

Rewards can provide a significant impetus for trade show attendees to participate in the survey. Researchers have had immense response by handing out golf or tennis balls, a free lunch, or another incentive to any end-users or potential end-users filling out a survey. In the case of individuals, focus groups stress the information sharing opportunity.

Focus Groups

Exhibitors often overlook the potential to set up end-user focus groups at trade shows. Focus group interviews can be applied to a variety of areas including product idea creation, concept exploration, and optimal market product positioning. Focus groups are frequently used to generate and refine product concepts and determine potential improvement areas of existing products.

You have several alternatives as you attempt to establish a trade show focus group. You can form the group before the show if you can acquire sufficient information on the end-users who will attend. The group can also be formed during the show. The most effective method is to station a screening team around the exhibition to identify and recruit appropriate end-users.

Standard focus groups require only 8 to 12 participants, but groups of 5 to 25 have been used for trade show research. The group should be designed to accurately reflect the characteristics of the market segment in which your research team is interested. Once the respondents are selected, take them to the chosen location and ask key questions about your product, their opinions of your company, and the marketplace. The following steps should be followed for a successful focus group.

- Establish rapport with the group — Attempt to structure the rules of group interaction while carefully outlining your objectives.

- Initiate discussion — Target your discussions among the group members in the areas in which you are interested.

- Carefully summarize the responses of the group — As you do this, you can determine the extent of consensus or conflict.

Written or Verbal Interviews

Interviews have emerged as an effective trade show research tool. While this survey technique is essentially similar to the questionnaire technique, interviews are less formal and generally more adaptable to the trade show environment. Some companies design their interview questions to encourage the end-user to walk around the exhibition booth while responding to questions on the product and company.

Written and verbal interviews can encourage potential customers to learn about new applications for products or to consider applications they may not have noticed. In addition, interviews can provide a variety of data possibly unobtainable from end-users simply visiting the booth.

Trade shows are possibly the best place to get immediate feedback about your product line. New product releases made in conjunction with trade shows can obtain maximum exposure for the product.

Get Immediate Feedback about New and Existing Products

A simple way to obtain feedback on your product is to ask the people attending your booth a series of questions. The questions asked should depend on whether the product is a totally new release or an improved existing model.

After identifying someone as a possible buyer or as having possible influence on the purchasing decision, ask a series of general questions and take notes for subsequent examination. Typical questions you might ask to acquire product feedback include:

- What product do you currently use?

- What problems (if any) are you having?

- If you are using one of our products now, how is it performing?

- How could the product be improved to better meet your needs?

- How could a new product better solve your problems?

Your existing product's performance can be estimated by asking end-users and potential end-users these questions. In addition, you can successfully form impressions about how your next product can better meet market needs.

Certain companies tie the majority of their trade show research to product introduction. This may be a little late since once your product is developed and introduced into the market, it can be difficult to implement recommendations of people attending trade shows.

Trade Show Research Can Help Develop Your Product

Trade show research should be concentrated during the product's developmental stage. Most trade show researchers highly recommend using marketing and product development staff on the show floor to determine optimal product features and likely markets. End-user suggestions can then be implemented into the design of new products (if appropriate) and proposed market strategy modified prior to product introduction.

Trade show research obtained during the product development stage can assist in determining optimal product packaging and presentation. Questioning distributors or retailers or both who attend trade shows and showing them proposed mock-ups of new product packaging can effectively improve packaging design. This strategy is particularly advisable for software companies that have met with considerable difficulty in successful product packaging.

Security Factors and Proprietary Information to Consider

When attempting to assemble research at the trade show, security factors and the proprietary information concerns of exhibitors should be a main concern.

Trade show exhibitors may attempt to protect what they consider proprietary information. Many exhibitors practice comprehensive lead-qualification procedures to accurately identify people entering their booth.

Increasing numbers of exhibitors are indicating that cameras and secretive research should be prohibited at trade shows unless specifically authorized by trade show management.

In Europe, trade show management efforts to adequately control secretive research activities are extremely stringent. Taking photographs in exhibitors' booths is usually strictly prohibited. Trade show security in the U.S. has been far more relaxed. The attitude has been that once you are at the trade show you are in the public domain. General indications are that security measures are on the increase as companies become more concerned about the flow of proprietary information.

Chapter 5

Successful Competitor Research Techniques

The primary goal of competitor research is to obtain an understanding of where your competitors are situated in the marketplace and to outline the likely strategic decisions a specific competitor or competitors might make.

Creating a detailed framework for competitive analysis enables you to develop a far more effective market and product development strategy. For you to create any type of detailed general business or specific marketing strategy, you should take some form of comprehensive and aggressive competitor analysis.

The objectives of competitor analysis should be apparent before beginning any competitor research process. Competitive analysis should consider possible and probable competitor responses to the entire range of potential strategic maneuvers your business might adopt. Competitive analysis should also try to indicate possible competitor reactions to any changes in industry structure and the general business environment, and to underlying economic or political fluctuations.

Competitor analysis should address several issues and answer a variety of questions about your competition and their related activities. Competitive analysis should try to determine the competitor's strategy and estimate the subsequent effects, if any, on your own company. Effective competitive analysis can assess the likely results of your entry into market niches or subsegments and potential competitor responses to your actions.

Surprisingly, competitive analysis is often not carried out at all or not done as thoroughly as it should be. Large companies allocating substantial funding for marketing often do extremely little in the way of competitor intelligence gathering. Even the most astute marketing executives have a tendency to assume that accurate competitor analysis is not possible, or that through competing with firms on a daily basis they know all they need to about the competitive strategies of those firms.

Competitor research in many companies is discouraged because of the difficulty in conducting in-depth competitor analysis and the amount of data required to accurately analyze competitor efforts. As a result, numerous companies competing in highly competitive marketplaces do not have a system to ensure systematic information gathering on their principal competitors. Decisions made regarding the future direction of competitor activities are based on intuition or piecemeal information assembled ad hoc.

A number of companies have recognized the value of competitive intelligence — or having a thorough knowledge and education of your competition — and have organized competitor intelligence gathering systems, usually within the domain of the market research group. If these systems are properly organized they can be extremely valuable and totally ethical.

Ethical issues are a primary concern of companies attempting to organize a system of competitive intelligence gathering. In the commercial world, corporate intelligence gathering goes on every day in some capacity and legal or ethical boundaries are rarely crossed.

The following section illustrates competitor intelligence system components, the correct way to establish a competitor intelligence framework, how to develop a system of competitive intelligence, and sources of competitor intelligence.

A Framework for Competitor Research

A few key factors can be used to assess a competitor's behavior. If these essential factors are kept in mind throughout the intelligence gathering process, the entire procedure can be simplified. Primary factors in competitor analysis are:

- Competitor objectives;

- Your competitor's existing methods;

- Competitor perceptions; and

- Competitor capacity.

An adequate understanding of these facets of a competitor's activity enables you to form ideas about competitor response to any stimulus, changes in the market, or the behavior of your own company. The majority of companies develop a feel for the methods of competitors, including the primary advantages and drawbacks of each. The competitors' underlying expectations and primary objectives are more difficult to assess, but a degree of understanding of these critical factors is vital for anticipating future swings in competitor behavior.

Determine which of your competitors should be analyzed before considering each of the previously outlined factors. Depending on your available resources and the size of your market, analyze four or five main competitors. Remember that each competitor is competing with you for some share of the market; so the impact of all competitors should be considered.

In addition to considering your existing competitors, use specific criteria to identify potential competition and their likely effects on your market, including:

- Companies competing in similar or related industries who could easily expand into your own market;

- Companies not hindered by entry barrier; or

- Existing distributors or end-users who might attempt to enter the market as a matter of convenience or cost-savings.

Changes in the competitive scene through acquisitions and mergers must be considered when assessing potential competition. To determine potential acquisition targets, consider:

- Capacity to endure drastic changes in the nature of the market;

- Current ownership; and

- Desirability to companies attempting to expand into or penetrate the market.

Set Up a Competitor Intelligence System

Publicly filed reports, newspaper and trade journal articles, statements by management or sales personnel, engineering estimates, and production schedules all represent potential competitor information sources.

Data becomes available in bits and pieces over time. An intricate, organized system should be developed for successful competitor intelligence gathering.

Design of a competitor intelligence system will vary depending on the type of industry, the particular company, staff capacity, and management. Figure 5-1 provides a basic outline of the potential structure, contents, and information flows of a competitor intelligence system. A number of design options are open depending on your specific requirements. The primary factor to consider when organizing your competitive information system is your specific staffing requirements.

In smaller markets or industries, one or two people can often effectively manage a competitor intelligence system. However, a single individual will usually have a hard time coping with the large volume of competitor intelligence sources and the responsibilities of gathering, sorting, and distributing data.

Different organizational strategies for the system have been adopted by varying companies, such as making the competitor intelligence group a subdivision of the corporate planning unit. Ideally, competitive intelligence should be drawn from a variety of departments and sources within the company.

Responsibility for the maintenance and organization of the competitive intelligence system should be delegated to an individual or group to avoid losing potentially valuable information. Regardless of the size of the company, competitor profiles should be required as part of the planning process. The size of the company and its capabilities should determine how comprehensive the system is and how many staff members are devoted to system management and maintenance.

Figure 5-1
How to Structure a Competitor Intelligence System

Collecting Data

Field Data Sources	**Published Data Sources**
• Salespeople	• Newspapers
• Engineers	• Government filings
• Market researchers	• and publications
• Distributors	• Trade journal articles
• Trade associations	• Patents

Sorting Data Alternatives
* Competitor files
* Source abstracts
* Computer filing of abstracts

Data Evaluation and Abstraction Alternatives
* Summaries
* Estimates of financial performance
* Summaries of annual reports
* Comparative financial performance
* Ranking of key competitors

Data Dissemination Alternatives
* Distribute as a competitive newsletter
* Situation or competitive status report
* Periodic reports to management

Data Utilization

Focus of Competitor Research

As you begin to research your competition, make sure you focus on four key elements. Take a close look at your competitor's:

- Capacity

- Objectives

- Perceptions

- Existing Methods

As you look at these four areas, you will begin to develop an overall picture of your competitor.

The first factor to use in competitive appraisal is the competitor's capacity. How the competitor approaches the market will be influenced by the competitor's existing methods, perceptions, and objectives in that market.

The extent of competitor reactions or initiatives is decided by their capacity, which can be determined by using the following seven factors.

- Product line — How broad is it?

- Research and development — Is there an extensive research and development facility and staff? What portion of total revenues is allocated to R&D?

- Company organization — Is the company organization tight and conducive to its perceived business strategy and objectives?

- Management — What is the quality and coordination capability of management? Does it exhibit a significant degree of flexibility in management style and response to external factors?

- Financial position — Profits, cash flows, capacity to generate credit, financial management track record — how well balanced are these factors in helping the company achieve financial goals?

- Distribution channels — What is the breadth of channels and their comparative quality and stability? Is follow-up product servicing adequate?

- Cost structure — What are the company's primary costs? Has it demonstrated a capability to adequately control and manage its costs in the past?

Assess competitor capacity in each of the seven areas. Has the company demonstrated any remarkable strengths or obvious weaknesses? Are there any significant indications that its strategy might change over time and, if so, what effect will this have on your approach to the competitor?

When assessing the competitive capacity of your competitors concentrate on:

- Their response rate to the competitive initiatives of others;

- Their ability to respond adequately to swings in external factors, such as the rate of inflation and rapid technological advancement; and

- Whether they have demonstrated any capacity to undertake and sustain a drawn-out, competitive situation with another company. If so, what were the primary strengths of the competitor during the battle — its management or its large reserves of cash?

An important point in competitor analysis is assessment of the competition's objectives. Understanding these objectives permits you to gauge the likelihood of changes in a competitor's strategies and potential reaction to changes in your behavior or alterations in market trends. If you are aware of the underlying objectives of a competitor, you can analyze the nature and effect of strategies the competitor might adopt.

Competitor objectives encompass financial, technical, market leadership, and general performance objectives. When attempting to determine the long-term objectives of a competitor, examine the relationship of the parent company (if there is one) to the operating unit in your market.

To get an idea of the potential impact of a company on the objectives of the operating unit, you can:

- Examine the operating unit of the company, which may comprise the entire company in certain instances; and

- Analyze its objectives, including those of the parent company.

Figure 5-2 provides a worksheet to help you assess the goals of competitor operating units.

Figure 5-2
Worksheet to Assess
Competitor Operating Objectives

Does the competitor hold any ideals that might affect its objectives? For example, does it want to be a market technology leader? _____

_____

How is the competitor organized? How is power allocated? Who makes decisions regarding pricing and product development? _____

_____

What are the major incentives? For example, what is the extent of executive compensation? What performance measures are in place at the company? _____

_____

What are the principal financial objectives of the competitor? _____

_____

Has the competitor demonstrated a willingness to take risks? _____

_____

What type of leaders make up management of the company? What appear to be their primary motivations? In particular, focus on putting together a profile on its Chief Executive Officer (CEO). _____

_____

What type of accounting system does the competitor use? How are prices set and costs analyzed? _____

_____

Do any regulations, such as antitrust laws, inhibit the actions of the competitor?____

_____

A detailed analysis of this information provides an excellent indication of the major objectives of your competitor's operating unit. Once its objectives are clearly understood, your competitor's reactions to your strategies and those of other competitors can be effectively mapped out and contingency plans drawn.

If the competitor you analyze is the operating unit of a larger corporate parent, this may affect the prediction of the competitor's objectives. The parent company may impose a variety of behavioral constraints on the operating unit that affect its reactions to various external influences, such as changes in your competitive strategy.

The worksheet in Figure 5-3 will aid in assessing the objectives of the parent company and resultant impacts of these objectives on the operating unit. An effective assessment of these factors will assist you in determining your competitor's primary objectives. This provides an indication of the likely strategies it might adopt and its responses to your strategic initiatives.

If your competitor is the operating unit of a highly diversified company, it can be rewarding to analyze the entire range of companies owned by the parent company.

Analyzing a competitor's goals helps you avoid stepping on your competitor's toes. You may be able to avoid changing your strategy and doing something to provoke increased competition and retaliation by your competitors.

In summary, analyzing the objectives of a competitor can provide valuable insight into desirable market strategies. With knowledge of the competitor's leading objectives, you can look for niches where your business can attempt to meet certain objectives without imposing on those of your competitors.

Competitor Perceptions

Another crucial segment of competitor analysis is identifying the underlying beliefs or perceptions of a competitor regarding itself, the market it competes in, and its own competitors.

All companies compete based on beliefs concerning their own role and performance in the market. These perceptions have a marked influence on the way a business competes in the market and its reactions to specific events.

Firms also compete on the basis of their perceptions regarding the entire industry and the companies contained within that industry. An examination of these perceptions can identify gaps or bias in perceptions of competing manufacturers about their company and the environment.

Identifying these gaps and biases can assist in finding competitive niches the competition may have previously ignored, allowing you to penetrate with a minimum of opposition. The worksheet in Figure 5-4 assists in identifying competitors' primary perceptions and the gaps and biases that may exist in those perceptions.

Past trends can provide an indication of competitor perceptions used in strategic planning and the objectives a competitor hopes to attain. Figure 5-5 provides a worksheet that will help you devise the historical business pattern of a competitor to determine its objectives and perceptions.

Figure 5-3
Worksheet to Assess the Effects of the Competitor Parent Company on the Objectives of the Operating Unit

Why did the parent company initially choose to enter the market? This will provide answers to the type of pressures being placed on the operating unit. _____

_____

Does the parent company place great emphasis on the importance of the operating unit as a component of its overall strategy? _____

_____

How is the parent company currently performing? Will performance trends on the part of the parent company result in increased pressure being placed on the operating unit? If the parent company is performing better than the operating unit this might be the case._____

_____

What are the primary objectives of the parent company? How does this affect the operating unit?_____

_____

Define the economic interaction between the parent company and the operating unit.

_____

How are operating unit managers compensated, provided with incentive, and controlled in relation to the parent company?_____

_____

Does the parent company apply a generic business strategy to all its operating units? If so, is it likely to be applied to your competitor?_____

_____

Are there any indications of further diversification plans by the parent company? If the parent company is moving into other areas, will this have any effect on the organization of the operating unit? _____

_____

What are the long-standing values or ideals of the parent company? Is it attempting to become a leader in all the markets in which it competes? _____

_____

How is the parent company organized? Does this provide an indication of the operating unit's standing in its corporate hierarchy? _____

_____

Does the operating unit maintain a relationship with any of the other operating units of the parent company, such as component supplier? _____

Figure 5-3 (continued)

What management characteristics appear to be rewarded by the parent company? Is it likely that the types of strategies advocated by these managers will be adopted across the board? _____

_____

Is the parent company controlled by any form of antitrust or other regulatory legislation that could overlap, thus affecting the objectives of the operating unit? _____

_____

Existing Methods

Methods used by the competition to approach the market need to be addressed when analyzing your competitors.

Focus on how your competitor currently operates. Determine the markets or niches on which it appears to concentrate and how it competes in those markets. For example, is the competitor competing primarily on the basis of price, or is it focusing on technological differentiation of products?

Other clues to existing perceptions and objectives of a company can be acquired by examining and assessing competitor management. Look closely at the managerial performance record in previous years or at other companies. Examine the factors most likely to impact managerial style and the success criteria management uses to assess its own performance.

Examining a manager's background can provide clues to the areas of competition he or she is likely to emphasize. Will he or she focus on marketing, product development, production, or distribution channels? The manager's background will most likely determine his or her focus points. For example, managers with an engineering background will most likely focus on close control of the production process for cost minimization.

All the elements of your competitor analysis can be brought together after completing your assessment of existing competitor methods. This provides an accurate picture of likely competitor responses to your competitive initiatives and the likely moves it may undertake.

Use the data you have compiled on competitor perceptions of the market and itself, its capacity, and its objectives, to assess potential initiatives your competition might undertake. Offensive action a competitor may take can be determined by comparing the competitor's goals to its current position in the market.

Competitive Research Data Sources

You can gather research on your competitors by using one of several ways. You can collect information via:

- Company literature,
- Company interviews,
- Government filings,
- Visual sightings,

- Plant inspections,
- Number of employees, or
- End-user history.

Company Literature

Companies publish a wide variety of literature about themselves. Generally, publicly traded companies produce more literature than private ones. Types of literature that can prove most valuable in competitive analysis are:

- Speeches or testimony made by company management,
- Company press releases,
- Product literature,
- End-user manuals,
- Annual meeting transcripts,
- Patent records,
- Product advertising, and
- Help wanted advertisements.

These sources can provide valuable information about competitor management objectives, the company's product offerings, and its perceptions of its role in the marketplace.

Company literature should be used for background information rather than data for specific or detailed analysis. Although literature released by a competitor will often contain a certain degree of bias and may prove misleading, it can help identify gaps in strategy or niches the competitor may have failed to exploit.

Competitor Interviews

Interviews with representative competitors can provide a wealth of competitive information. Detailed information on market and technical trends, production schedules, strategic planning, and product development can be extracted during a telephone conversation with a willing competitor employee. Product or sales managers can prove particularly informative.

Companies are generally unwilling to divulge any proprietary information to their closest competitors for obvious reasons. To interview members of your competitor's organization under an assumed identity is highly unethical and may even cross the boundaries of legality.

An honest information exchange may prove an alternative. Your primary competitors may be as interested to find out about you as you are about them and may readily agree to an information sharing session. As this can be detrimental to your own competitive position, the solution to the competitor interview problem generally lies with an unbiased third party.

A market research company may be commissioned to conduct competitor interviews. Companies are often willing to discuss proprietary issues with an independent company preparing an overview of the entire industry. This is possibly the only way to acquire highly sensitive competitive data from your primary competitors without crossing ethical lines.

Figure 5-4
Worksheet to Assess Competitor Perceptions

What perceptions, if any, does the competitor appear to have regarding its position in the market? Use the statements of management and salespeople to discern this information. Are these perceptions accurate? _____

_____

Does the competitor exhibit a significant degree of faith in historical trends? How does this affect product design, distribution, and so on? _____

_____

Does the competitor appear to have any perceptions concerning long-term demand trends and the potential impact of current industry trends? Is the competitor going to be likely to under- or overproduce? _____

_____

Do any regional or cultural issues appear to affect competitor perceptions? _____

_____

Does the company organization or structure appear in any way to influence its perceptions of itself or the current market? _____

_____

Does the competitor appear to place a great deal of faith in the existing consensus of opinion in the industry regarding future trends and events? _____

_____

Clues to the perceptions of a competitor are likely to be contained in its current strategies. Issues affecting the company at present may be used as the cornerstone for its perceptions of the future. _____

_____

Does the competitor appear to have any preconceptions about the expected behavior of its competitors? Does it have a tendency to under/overestimate them? If so, how can this be used to your advantage? _____

_____

Government Filings

Government filings, particularly annual reports, can provide competitor information and should be consulted early in your competitive assessment. A quick look through the annual reports of ten of the leading firms in an industry can provide insight into the prevailing intensity of competition.

Underlying reasons for satisfactory or unsatisfactory financial results given in an annual report can provide examples of the reasons for competitive success or failure. Annual reports can also provide indications of a company's perceptions of itself in the industry and its long-term objectives.

Figure 5-5
Worksheet to Use Historical Trends
to Indicate Competitor Perceptions and Objectives

Has the competitor had a history of success in the marketplace? Has the company had a history of failure? Are there any indications that the track record of the competitor is influencing its approach to the market or itself? _____

_____

What has been your competitor's greatest strength historically? Is it a proven technology leader? Has it always maintained a large market share? Is the competitor likely to continue its attempt to lead in these areas? _____

_____

Does the competitor have a set piece reaction to certain competitive initiatives? Is it likely to behave in a similar way in the future? _____

_____

How does the competitor's current financial standing in the market and its total share compare to that of the recent past? Is it greater or less? What does this tell you about the competitor's goals and its capacity to achieve them? _____

_____

Other government filings such as SEC forms, regulatory filings, 10-Ks, prospectuses, and proxy statements can provide useful insights into the financial state of your primary competitors.

Visual Sightings

Visual sightings are an effective way to monitor competitor activities. Observations on the size of your competitor's main manufacturing plant and total parking facilities provide an excellent indication of its manufacturing capacity and total number of employees.

This technique should be used in conjunction with other available methods to assess the competition. For example, if your literature search indicates that one of your major competitors has been laying off employees, a quick scan of the corporate parking lot can provide a reasonable employee head count to confirm your suspicions.

Plant Inspections

Inspecting a competitor's plant can reveal a great deal about their activities. For example, expanding plant facilities for storage or manufacturing can indicate possible expansion of a competitor's production schedule in subsequent periods; expanded parking facilities can indicate that the firm has taken on additional employees. The total size and shape of a plant may indicate very little to you, but could tell your engineers a great deal about a competitor's production process. For example, is the process capital- or labor-intensive?

Noting a competitor's sales office location(s) can reveal where the company's sales are concentrated and regional markets the company is pursuing.

As previously indicated, head counts or counting the total number of parking spaces outside your competitor's plant can reveal a great deal about your competitor's workforce and hiring processes.

Examining want ads can provide insight into the personnel a competitor might need and information about its potential market strategy.

After estimating total employees, use an employee-to-square-foot-of-plant ratio to check the accuracy of the estimates.

Number of Employees

A potentially good source of competitive information is your competitor's dissatisfied customers. Several companies have developed databases using information from their competitor's dissatisfied customers. This information was subsequently used very effectively in competing for new sales.

Competitor End-user History

Figure 5-6 presents an example of a competitor profile. The profile is a segment of a large, detailed, industry competitive analysis providing detailed information regarding the competitor's product offerings, financial background, and strategy.

This type of competitor profile is an excellent way to present the results of competitor analysis to company product and marketing decision makers. The profile is brief but encompasses all the main points of the competitor's operations and summarizes them concisely. If competitor profiles and their activities are formulated, updated, and passed on to relevant executives on a periodic basis, the decision making process becomes more informed and directed toward meeting existing competitive environment demands.

Presenting Results of Competitor Analysis

Figure 5-6
Detailed Competitor Profile

SYDIS, Inc.
410 East Plumeria Dr.
San Jose, CA 95134
408/945-1100

Contacts John Clark, President
Kenneth Gilbert, Director of Product Marketing
William Stensrud, V.P. of Marketing

Financial Background

Sydis was founded in February, 1989, receiving $2.75 million in a first round of venture financing from Merrill, Pickard, Anderson & Eyre, Asset Management, and New Enterprises Associates. In June 1990, Sydis received $10 million in additional financing from the original investors and new investors such as General Electric Venture Capital Corporation and Citicorp Venture Capital Fund Limited Partnership.

Headed by former Philips C.E.O. John Clark, the company displayed its first working prototype in May 1991 and installed its first Voice Station System (VSS) in June 1992. The company is privately held with no present plans for going public.

Product Offerings

VSS including VoiceStation 1 (IVDT) and Information Manager (Minicomputer), VoiceStation 110 (IVDT Micro Add-on).

Product Analysis

The Voice Station System (VSS) is a Unix-based, multi-user mini-computer that was the first IVDT type of product to incorporate the use of digitized voice features. The VSS, because of its superior use of such features backed up with a powerful multi-user computer was, until the introduction of Santa Barbara Labs' Centerpoint, the only product with a large enough memory storage capacity to allow full use of digitized voice storage.

At the center of the VSS is an information manager providing all standard office applications software and development tools, newly added GKS-based business graphics, and all voice/data communications facilities. In addition, the actual IVDT section of the system is the VoiceStation 1 and the newly added VoiceStation 110, which converts an IBM PC or DEC VT-100 compatible into a full functioning voice/data terminal.

Figure 5-6 (continued)

The VoiceStation's use of graphic icons, extensive windowing, and well-positioned, easy-to-use "soft" keys make it appealing to many non-computer-literate users. Managers and others who spend the majority of their time on the telephone can use most of the VoiceStation 1's features without learning to use the optional key-board. If a keyboard is needed for word processing or other functions, the VoiceStation's key-board meets the basic DIN ergonomic specifications.

The VSS concept is centered around the idea of providing total office communications ability for executives and their staffs. For the VSS to achieve its full capabilities, the secretary and the manager should have VoiceStations on their desks. With the intro-duction of the VoiceStation 110, the worker who does not necessarily need the elabo-rate VoiceStation 1, or who already has an IBM PC on his desk, can become part of the VSS network through the local area network, called Sylink. Purchasers can decide which kind of terminal will best suit the specific needs of the people in divergent areas of the company. With the addition of the VoiceStation 110, Sydis has helped make the VSS more adaptable to existing office environments.

Sydis can take substantial credit for the systems-oriented approach to solving the office communications/automation dilemma. Although it was not the first to market a multi-user IVDT (Davos was the first), it has demonstrated what is, so far, the most compre-hensive approach to the voice/data communications problem. Future IVDTs will likely exhibit similar features.

Company Strategy

As one of the first companies to offer a truly advanced IVDT system, Sydis has faced a difficult battle in gaining market acceptance for its products. It has had to overcome the initial misconception (because of its appearance) that it is just another IVDT. Its high price, which averages around $6,500 per station (including the Information Manager), has been an inhibiting factor to the firm's gaining any foothold in the market.

The VSS has been designed to accommodate up to 64 users per controller but it can be run efficiently with fewer stations on line. In fact, VSSs sold thus far have averaged only 8 users per system. With the introduction of the VoiceStation 110, future sales will probably show more users on line. This could help reduce average purchase price by distributing the cost of the expensive Information Manager throughout the office. Instead of purchasing the VoiceStation 1 units at $3,500 each, a VoiceStation 110 could be purchased for $600 and interfaced with an existing PC or VT-100 compatible terminal.

Sydis stresses the major emphasis of the VSS is not the VoiceStation itself but rather the VSS behind it. Although the capacity to employ PCs instead of VoiceStation 1s may reduce revenue per system sale, the important thing to Sydis is selling the total system. Anything that can make the system more appealing will be implemented.

Figure 5-6 (continued)

Sydis is distributing the VSS primarily through OEM/VAR arrangements. The most notable of these is the $145 million OEM contract with GTE Business Communications Systems, signed in January 1984. Sydis' financial success in the coming year will hinge primarily upon whether or not the GTE name will gain market acceptance for the VSS. Except on a preexisting interconnect reseller contract with ComPath National calling for minimum purchases of $21 million over five years, Sydis has agreed to grant GTE exclusive U.S. rights to distribute the VSS to companies with PBX-based applications. Sydis continues to work with potential non-PBX VARs in tailoring the system for vertical markets, including such functions as client billing and records, as well as the ability to keep electronic copies of X-rays on line.

The Sydis management, like others in the industry, is looking forward to introductions of similar systems by IBM and AT&T. It has covered a long road trying to gain acceptance for a product that so far has experienced good reviews but few sales. It believes that the introduction of voice/data products by the "big-players" will give the voice/data concept much-needed market acceptance. Many believe that even with increased market acceptance for voice/data products the VSS may be too expensive for the existing market to bear.

Chapter 6

Proven Customer Research Techniques

End-user Surveys

End-user surveys are one of the most efficient ways to determine end-user perceptions of your company and to get an accurate idea of your company's image. The relevance of end-user information to the customer can be segmented into the following two distinct categories:

- Data that is valuable to the marketing group; and
- Data that is valuable to the product development function.

Detailed information about end-users in your marketplace provides the basic platform for all marketing decisions.

Marketing decision makers need descriptive information about their markets. How many end-users are there? What are total potential unit and dollar sales in each segment of the overall market? You need to know your company's comparative ranking in the total market and in each discrete market segment. The most important factors to be aware of are the relevant objectives and needs of end-users and how these objectives might best be served by your products.

End-user surveys are a direct way to acquire reliable information on the beliefs, attitudes, and perceptions of customers and potential customers. Another way to obtain end-user information is the sales monitoring method. Sales monitoring methods are basically a form of trial and error involving the placement of new products and the accrual of customer feedback. This is a haphazard way to acquire customer information and can prove expensive, particularly if the product does not sell well and is not fulfilling a great need among end-users.

In previous years, product design and development was comparatively straightforward. The trend among manufacturers was to expect end-users to adapt to the requirements of the particular product. After the completion of the design phase, the development stage was considered complete except for any modifications that became necessary due to design flaws.

In today's competitive environment all companies should organize a market research group and devote significant funding to research and development to ensure profits and maintain a competitive edge. The primary objectives of the product development process are:

- To develop a product representing a better solution to end-user problems than the products offered by competitors.

- To devise superior products to those of your competition. To do this, the product design and development group must be oriented to meet the requirements and wants of end-users.

- To acquire extensive ideas from end-users. By paying close attention to the complaints and requests of end-users, you can learn where your products are lacking and formulate plans to meet previously unforeseen end-user needs.

Using end-user surveys can save money and help ensure that product promotion, price, and placement programs are optimally executed. Three basic methods for completing end-user surveys are:

- Telephone

- Mail

- Personal interviews

These techniques and methods can be easily applied to customer research to identify predominant trends in end-user opinions and market demand direction. Interviews with end-users, whether conducted through mail surveys, in person, or over the telephone, can be vital sources of information. Advantages of end-user interviews include the following:

- During a telephone or personal interview, end-users will often express significant opinions that they would often be unwilling to put down on paper (even in an anonymous mail survey).

- Honest product appraisals can be secured and are a vital means of improving your company's performance. Dissatisfied end-users will often turn to a competitor's product if your offering does not adequately meet their needs.

- Personal and telephone interviews afford the added advantage of being able to catch verbal inflections and facial expressions of respondents. These subtleties can tell a great deal about an end-user or potential end-user's opinion of your product.

First-hand information from end-users of your product is essential for any marketing executive. Telephone and personal interviews afford added advantages in end-user surveying because they enable the interviewer to accumulate accurate ideas about the objectives of potential end-users and determine exactly what their product demands are. A perceptive interviewer can learn a great deal more from this kind of contact than from published secondary data on trends in end-user demand and behavior.

Remember to structure interview questions to encourage end-users to articulately express their feelings. Try to get them to talk about your product line, marketing strategy, company, the competitor's product offering, and what they consider ideal product features.

Dissatisfied customers can tell you a great deal more than your sales people. Listening to the opinions and perceptions of your sales people is a fairly effective way to pick up customer information but feedback from sales people is often biased. Furthermore, the information you receive reflects the current needs of end-users and not their potential requirements.

A focus group interview involves bringing a small group of respondents together for in-depth group interviewing. Focus group interviews are very different from individual interviews. Information flows are not as closely guided between respondent and interviewer. Opinions of members of the focus group are discussed by all group members, giving rise to informative and topical data.

Focus Groups

During the focus group interview, the interviewer becomes more of a moderator than an interviewer. Focus groups are an extremely effective method of market research and are increasingly utilized as a customer research technique. End-user data derived through focus group interviews can:

- Provide new ideas for the potential improvement of existing products;

- Provide new product design concepts;

- Give insight into the likelihood of the success or failure of a particular marketing strategy; and

- Identify the product performance requirements of the end-user and needs that are not currently being met.

Focus groups involving end-users can be used to evaluate proposed marketing strategies or advertising material. Design of the focus group is essential in determining its eventual success or failure. When designing focus groups, consider the following issues:

- The principle consideration when organizing a group should be its size. Small groups can be easily dominated by an over-zealous moderator or a forceful group member.

- Individual screening interviews should be used to ensure that no group member has any overwhelming biases or preconceptions that may adversely affect the direction of the interview.

- A typical focus group interview with end-users should last from 90 to 120 minutes.

- The interview site is important and should be as neutral and nonthreatening as possible.

- The interview should be recorded for subsequent transcription and analysis.

The moderator is an essential factor in an effective focus group interview. The moderator must ensure that 1) all predetermined objectives of the focus group interview are met; 2) lead the discussion; and 3) make sure no degree of personal bias affects the interview. The free flow of ideas and information among group members must be encouraged as this is the key to the success of the interview. Some desirable features of a moderator are:

- The moderator must show enthusiasm in the topic or the group will lose interest.

- The moderator must be able to convey a lack of understanding of respondent answers to encourage members of the group to discuss concepts in greater detail.

- The moderator must be able to encourage some controversy among the respondents to generate deeper discussion, but cannot allow the interview to degenerate into argument.

- The moderator must be able to encourage involvement by all members of the group.

- The moderator must be able to simultaneously exhibit significant empathy with the group while remaining firm enough to maintain close control over the interview.

- The moderator must be adaptable. Prior to the interview, the moderator should memorize the questionnaire and allow the session to flow without enforcing an arbitrary question order.

- The moderator must be responsive to the focus group members' sensitivities. He or she needs to pay close attention to the group's emotional responses to certain issues, which may conflict with their expressed opinions. It is often essential for the moderator to read between the lines to uncover information.

Focus group interviews of a representative group of end-users offer certain advantages over the individual interview format. However, interpreting results is often difficult and interview moderation cumbersome. Because responses are unstructured, any formal tabulation of results is complicated. Therefore, focus group end-user interviews are generally ideally suited to exploratory interviews when attempting to discover new ideas rather than analyze them. Focus group end-user interviews are being used to provide the basic ideas for product concepts and a broad evaluation of optimal market positioning.

Advantages of End-user Focus Groups

- Opinions or ideas of individual group members can be refined by the group, resulting in more accurate information.

- The "snowballing" factor can occur, causing individual ideas of group members to pass around and gather both momentum and detail.

- Focus group interviews are generally more interesting to the respondent than individual interviews. As a result, answers may be longer and more revealing.

- Since the moderator's questions are directed at a group as opposed to individuals, the spontaneity of answers is often greater.

Disadvantages of End-user Focus Groups

- As focus groups often last from two to three hours and must take place at a central location, securing the cooperation of a random sample is often difficult.

- Structuring a random sample is complicated. Participants in the interview are likely to be different from those not participating. So non-response can be a serious problem.

- Focus groups are generally more costly than other end-user interview alternatives.

- If the moderator fails to ask certain questions or delve deeply into specific areas, significant biases can be introduced into the proceedings. The potential for errors, due to moderator-introduced bias, is significant.

- Skilled moderators are difficult to find and their services are often expensive.

Focus groups can provide excellent customer research information, presenting a unique opportunity to assemble a group of end-users and potential end-users to discuss their unique needs, objectives, and perceptions. Opinions and statements of the respondents should feed each other and provide interesting information for drawing conclusions.

Beta Sites

Beta sites are a form of product use testing; a step between the laboratory and the placement of any product on the market. The goal of most companies is timely general release of the best product possible, and beta site testing can reveal strengths and weaknesses of a product without unduly postponing market introduction.

Beta site testing, the second step in the end-user testing cycle, involves actual preliminary use of the product by a carefully selected sample group of end-users representative of the market you intend to serve. Alpha site testing, the initial phase, involves placing a single product prototype with an end-user for a period of time. The principal shortcomings overlooked in laboratory testing are generally revealed during alpha site testing and the prototype improved for beta site testing.

Beta site field testing involves placing several products at a number of end-user sites for a specified time period. Day-to-day use of the product at these testing sites generally reveals the majority of design flaws and manufacturing problems related to the product. These drawbacks may then be rectified before general product release.

Analyzing the efficiency of a new product entails a great deal more than selecting the target market. Beta sites assist in determining the needs of the targeted market segment and features your product must have for it to perform adequately and meet market needs.

Beta site testing is a highly desirable form of use testing as it provides a significant amount of customer information at comparatively low costs. Occasionally, two or more versions of the product may be provided to different beta sites to test end-user preferences for alternative product configurations or features.

Test Marketing

Test marketing is a marketing experiment conducted in a small, carefully chosen segment of the total marketplace. Test marketing has expanded rapidly since the early 1960s as a customer research tool. The primary goals of test marketing are:

- To predict sales and profit impacts of proposed market planning or strategy changes;
- To market new products or enhanced versions of existing products; and
- To determine the potential reaction of end-users.

Test marketing is not limited to testing likely end-user reaction to new product release. The efficiency of all elements of the marketing mix can be determined via sales testing.

Often the test marketing program structure will mirror a planned national or regional marketing program for the product, but on a more limited scale and geographic scope.

The test marketing process involves variations in different marketing mix variables. Management can assess test marketing results to determine the optimal blend of marketing mix variables for general product introduction. The primary applications of test marketing include:

- New product enhancements,
- Proposed product price changes,
- Alterations in distribution and advertising, and
- Alerting management to previously undetected product design flaws or drawbacks.

Two widely used types of test marketing exist — standard test marketing and controlled test marketing.

In standard market tests, a sample area or areas are selected when the product is sold utilizing common distribution channels. A number of marketing mix combinations may be employed and the variables manipulated to determine the optimal choice.

The test marketing mix is generally used with an end-user survey to determine the results of various marketing mixes utilized and their impact on the test's market. Standard test marketing can have significant drawbacks. The main disadvantages of the standard test marketing format are:

- Competitors often vary their own marketing mix by lowering prices or raising advertising expenditures in an effort to disrupt your test marketing results.

- Competitors can be alerted to your new product by your test marketing program. They can counter by working on a competing product or modifying their market strategy to minimize the impact of your new release.

- Competitors can often glean as much information from your test marketing program as you can. If a competitor manages to read your test marketing program results, it can successfully restructure to defeat your general product release.

- Test marketing programs can be extremely expensive.

Standard Test Marketing

Controlled market tests can overcome the difficulties associated with standard marketing tests by, among other things, using a market research company to handle marketing mix elements, such as storage and pricing distribution. The research company typically test-markets the product at fewer sites, reducing the potential for competitors to become aware of the test.

The primary advantages and disadvantages of controlled market tests are summarized below.

Controlled Test Marketing

Advantages of Controlled Market Testing

- Tests can be quickly completed.

- A greater degree of competitive security is offered.

- It is less costly than standard market testing.

Disadvantages of Controlled Market Testing

- Lack of distribution — channel use impacts test reality.

- Nonutilization of intended distribution channels prohibits testing an element of the marketing mix.

It is unlikely that controlled market testing will completely replace standard market tests. Rapid increases in controlled market testing indicates that it will retain its current role as a useful supplement to standard market testing.

In recent years, a great deal of attention has been paid to applying computer simulation to market testing. Computer simulation involves creating a model designed to resemble a real series of processes or an operating system.

Computer Simulation

Experiments can then be performed using the model to accumulate better knowledge about the way the system functions. The greatest possible application would be to develop a model of the marketplace so exacting that computer simulation testing could be as accurate as standard market testing. The net effect would be a marked reduction in total costs and complete security from potential competitive retaliation.

The complexity of the majority of markets frequently makes it necessary to employ a computer for market simulation. Computer simulation is generally applicable for certain specific market types. Markets are highly adaptable for computer simulation if:

- The processes and systems underlying the market are simple enough to easily lend themselves to model construction; and

- Relevant market data required to create the models is readily available and leading market indicators tend to be comparatively stable over time.

Computer simulations for market testing are generally most applicable to tests addressing product distribution, promotion, and pricing alternatives. Product release tests and comprehensive variations of marketing mix variables are usually less applicable to computer simulation.

While computer simulation is applicable in creating market models for test marketing experimentation, conventional methods are generally applicable to a larger number of actual situations.

Cost Structure

All types of marketing experiments are expected to see increased use over time. If the research problem involves selecting one of a given set of available market strategies, market experiments will be used increasingly to assist management decision making.

Test marketing benefits should always be considered along with the costs. The costs of test marketing are generally insignificant when compared to overall product development and marketing costs — a failed marketing program will cost substantially more that a test marketing program.

The three primary problems generally associated with all forms of marketing experiments, including test marketing, are:

- Budget constraints,

- Time constraints, and

- Control difficulties.

Budgeting has always been the primary difficulty associated with test marketing programs. The costs of this type of marketing experiment may be divided into direct and indirect costs.

Standard research costs arise from:

- Design of data collection methods,

- Design of the sample, and

- Wages of field staff conducting research.

The direct costs of research in a test marketing program are often substantial. Test marketing should mirror closely the national or regional marketing plan, so indirect costs should also be considered. Potential indirect costs of a realistic test marketing program consist of:

- Marketing costs,
- Sales costs, and
- Costs of promotional literature and displays.

If the marketing test assesses the likely success or failure of a new product introduction, a further series of potential costs must be considered in developing the test marketing program. Production costs must be accounted for and the extent of production required calculated on the basis of potential production costs. The necessary production schedule for the test marketing program can be calculated by examining the total potential market and calculating the required test market size.

Time constraints represent a potential problem in using test marketing as a means of surveying customers. Depending on the type of market or product being considered, it often requires up to twelve months for a decision based upon the results of the test marketing program. Elements affecting required time factors in a test marketing program are:

- Potential seasonal sales fluctuations,
- Repeat buying behavior, and
- Total product life cycle.

The temptation to undertake a lengthy test market program, considering a host of potential variables, is often high. Lengthy experiments may likely increase costs substantially and only provide slight additional information. Long market tests can exacerbate test control problems and the potential for competitor reaction.

The primary consideration in determining potential costs of the test marketing program should be the weight of perceived costs against perceived benefits.

Rarely do you have a second chance to improve a product after its general introduction — either it hits or it misses. A properly conducted market test can be critical both in avoiding costs and saving time.

Notes

Section 3

Tools and

T E C H N I Q U E S

Chapter 7

Forecasting: An Effective Research Tool

Forecasting — a tool used in the decision making process — involves the accumulation of baseline sales data for use in projecting future trends. By providing an indication of what might occur, forecasts offer the opportunity to select alternative courses of action.

Definition and Role

It is important to understand the limitations of forecasting. The market forecast can be beneficial in day-to-day decision making, despite two primary limitations.

- It is impossible to accurately predict future events. All forecast methods depend on some degree of judgment rather than fact.

- Gaps will always appear in forecasts. No forecast, regardless of how comprehensive, can account for all potential future events.

All marketing decisions depend on a certain degree of sales forecasting to assess the market potential of existing and potential products.

In most corporate structures the market research group is responsible for forecast data. Many companies currently undertake routine long- and short-term forecasting.

For a firm tracking market direction, sales and market forecasting should be the cornerstone of all your business' primary decisions. The key areas where market and sales forecasts are used for decision making include:

- Determining personnel requirements;

- Defining finance budgets;

- Identifying production schedules and budgets;
- Evaluating marketing strategy;
- Appraising investments; and
- Assessing the need for new market strategies and product development.

The extent of company or industry operations depends upon existing and potential sales available in the marketplace. An accurate sales and market forecast enables you to define targets and objectives and identify the most efficient way to achieve these targets in the short-, medium-, and long-term.

At one time market forecasting was viewed as an extremely complicated process reliant on developing complex models and statistical analysis methods. Typically, managers requiring forecasts lack the time, financial resources, and data to build complicated statistical models for forecasting purposes.

Types of Forecasting Data

While practically any marketing variable can be forecast over time, market forecasts are predominantly based on three types of forecasting data:

- Sales volume data at current prices,
- Base year sales volume and price data, and
- Unit sales.

Sales Volume at Current Prices

Sales volume data at current prices is the total sales volume at currently prevailing market prices. This data does not take into account expected future fluctuations in prices and the long-term effects of inflation.

Base Year Sales Volume and Price Data

Base year sales volume and price data are sales volume values related to prevailing prices over a particular sales period. The period selected is referred to as the base period and sales in subsequent periods in the series under consideration are calculated based on the values or prices of that base period.

The principal advantage of this method is that it removes the effects of inflationary price increases over the period, providing a market forecast measured in "real" terms.

Unit Sales

Unit sales measure total units sold over a period of time. This method of accumulating forecast data avoids problems encountered with fluctuating prices and inflation. This method limits forecasting on the total market or company level when the units being measured are comparatively uniform. Unit sales may be compared against sales at current period prices to determine comparable market price sensitivity. Both unit and price can be combined to forecast the future.

Historical comparisons of unit sales, base year sales volume, and price and sales volume data at current prices allow identification of sensitive relationships.

Further analysis can produce crucial facts that can influence the direction of the forecasts. Plotting value percentage increases or decreases between periods allows you to project and trend forecast data well into the future.

For a valid forecast, all the forecast data types described should be analyzed and projected. If you are researching a broader-based market containing a variety of products, each market segment should be forecast individually using the data described previously to gain an accurate picture of sales in all market segments and subsegments.

Forecasting Techniques

The basic market forecasting techniques currently used are:

- Judgment methods,
- Time series analysis and projection, and
- Informal methods.

Judgmental Forecasting

Market forecasting involves a certain degree of judgment. Forecasting methods fall under specific judgmental categories when the method used cannot be adequately detailed to allow reproducible results. The three basic methods of judgmental forecasting are the:

- Expert consensus method,
- Delphi method, and
- Aggregation of sales personnel forecasts.

Expert Consensus Method. Expert consensus is a widely used method of judgmental forecasting. Experts frequently called upon to prepare forecasts include:

- Company executives,
- Market researchers,
- Trade association personnel,
- Government agency representatives, and
- Industry consultants.

Obtaining forecasts from experts, however, can be difficult. Figure 7-1 provides a methodology for obtaining a sales forecast from an industry expert.

In this example, the analyst obtained a market estimate from an industry expert who originally disclaimed awareness of annual sales in the market. Note that the estimate was not just given to the researcher to satisfy him or her — a range was developed and narrowed until a reasonably accurate figure was determined.

An expert has estimates of the probability of sales reaching certain levels. The real skill of an analyst is to coerce experts into stating their estimates, then get them to use their expertise to narrow the estimate range.

Figure 7-1
A Dialogue to Obtain a Sales Forecast from an Industry Expert

Researcher: Could you give me an estimate of annual sales?

Marketing Executive: I really am not sure. However, I feel sales will be quite strong.

Researcher: Is it your opinion that sales will exceed $20 million this year?

Marketing Executive: That's doubtful.

Researcher: Do you believe that sales will exceed $12 million?

Marketing Executive: Now that is quite likely.

Researcher: Could sales fall as low as $6 million a year?

Marketing Executive: No way. If that was a possibility we would not have entered the market.

Researcher: Would you place sales at around $9 million then?

Marketing Executive: If anything, I would estimate that as a fraction low.

Researcher: In the light of that, at what level would you place sales?

Marketing Executive: I would put them at approximately $10 million annually.

Delphi Method. The Delphi method seeks to achieve group consensus but avoids problems associated with expert consensus by engaging the experts in anonymous debate. As a researcher, you act as an intermediary for exchanging the experts' opinions, thus avoiding unfair weighting of individual expert forecasts and bias introduced during a joint forecast.

The Delphi forecasting method may be broken into a series of processes.

- Step 1 – The participating experts create separate forecasts.

- Step 2 – The forecasts are returned to the analyst to weigh them.

- Step 3 – The combined forecast formulated by the analyst is returned to the industry experts.

- Step 4 – The experts compile a new series of forecasts based upon the combined data.

- Step 5 – The procedure is continued until no greater degree of consensus is achievable.

The premise of the Delphi method is that subsequent estimates provided by the experts will be less dispersed. The median response of the group provides an indication of the optimum forecast.

The Delphi forecasting method has been successfully applied to short-, medium-, and long-range forecasting for both existing and newly released products. The Delphi method has also been used in long-term technology forecasting.

Aggregation of Sales Personnel Forecasts. Aggregating sales personnel forecasts is one of the oldest and most widely used judgmental sales forecasting techniques. The method is simple to perform and involves questioning sales representatives to obtain their sales projections over a specified period. The comparative advantages are:

- Its inexpensiveness, and

- Its short-term accuracy.

The comparative disadvantages include:

- Its difficulty to encourage sales personnel to generate an accurate sales forecast based on realistic expectations.

- Its difficulty to account for the optimistic or pessimistic biases of sales personnel when analyzing the data. (To account for bias, you must conduct ongoing comparison between forecast data and actual sales figures for the relevant period.)

While sales personnel may be aware of expected fluctuations in the buying patterns of end-users, they are often ignorant of other factors that may impact the forecast.

The accuracy of sales personnel forecasts is generally restricted to the short-term since underlying economic factors are beyond their immediate concerns.

Companies using aggregate individual forecasts of sales personnel for market forecasting have developed methods to improve the accuracy of the forecasts. You can:

- Discuss salespersons' forecasting performance records with them before having them conduct the forecast.

- Provide sales personnel an overview forecast of the general business outlook for the period.

- Discuss the forecast with each individual salesperson before its submission.

The second basic market forecasting technique, time series analysis and projection, is relatively simple to incorporate into your marketing plan.

Time Series Analysis and Projection

Time series forecasts closely analyze a certain variable such as commodity unit or dollar sales. The arrangement of the variable in relation to time is closely observed.

Time series analysis forecasting relies on the assumption that observed fluctuations in a variable in preceding periods may be used to forecast future trends in that variable. For example, if a plot of commodity unit sales follows a particular pattern over the past five observed periods, this pattern or trend may be projected to similar future periods.

A time series usually comprises four distinct cycles of fluctuations or variations, including:

- Seasonal
- Cycle
- Trend
- Random

Seasonal variations — fluctuations under a year — occur on a periodic basis. An example of a seasonal variation is the peak in sales of children's clothing and footwear before the start of a school year.

Cycle variations refer to any fluctuations observed to last more than a year. An accurate prediction of cycle variations is difficult because they do not occur with any kind of regularity.

Trend variations are distinct, long-term patterns underlying the overall growth, decline, or stability of the market. An individual company's sales over time will show considerable fluctuation in response to swings in demand or market competition.

Random variations can impact time series forecasts. They occur because of statistically unforeseeable factors, such as political or social unrest and unprecedented economic occurrences.

Use a Time Series Graph. When forecasting market or sales growth by company or industry it is often good to start by plotting variables such as dollar sales or commodity unit sales on a time series graph.

Many time series forecasting models are available. Widely used methods include:

- Exponential smoothing,
- Statistical trend analysis,
- Naive model forecasts, and
- Moving average models.

The exponential smoothing method formulates a weighted moving average. The more recent the observed variable, the heavier the weight attached to it. The reasoning is that when forecasting sales, the most recent sales are likely to provide the most accurate predictions of sales likely in the next period.

Statistical trend analysis requires determining the fundamental growth trend pattern or the stability or decline of the series being analyzed.

Naive model forecasts involve total reliance on last period sales trends to indicate the next period's sales. Accurate forecasts can be achieved if the overall forecast is flat and the effects of variations minimal.

Moving average models rely on averaging the values of the preceding number of periods. The average is constantly updated. Each period moves as the value of another sales period is included in the average and the value of period X + 1 is no longer used.

Using these models can be complicated and cumbersome. The statistical basis needed to make the model work is not always available. It can be easier to acquire historical data via the expert consensus method and use expert opinions to project perceived future trends.

If the dependent variables can be selected from the independent variables, how these independent variables have behaved in the past can be observed and projected onto subsequent periods. Examples of trend projection are presented in Figures 7-2 and 7-3.

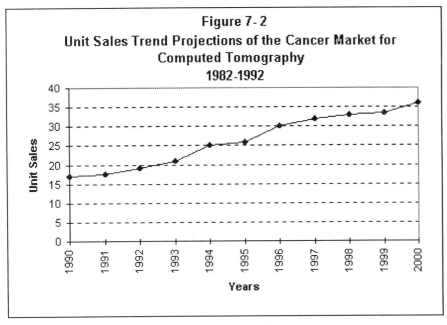

Figure 7-2

Unit Sales Trend Projections of the Cancer Market for Computed Tomography

1982-1992

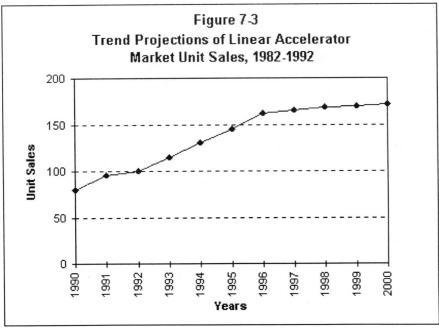

Figure 7-3

Trend Projections of Linear Accelerator Market Unit Sales, 1982-1992

Plotting trend projections, as shown in Figures 7-2 and 7-3, can assist in molding forecast numbers into a coherent visual form. Visual presentation can help identify general trends, seasonal demand patterns and variations from typical patterns.

The implication of history proving repetitive is often accurate in terms of end-user demand. As demand patterns for certain products are repetitive, certain markets are more stable than others over time.

If recurring demand patterns can be identified, the potential forecasting application is marked. Several principal drawbacks of trend projection exist, including:

- Trend projection relies on the assumption that previous forces affecting the market will continue to do so in the future.

- Relationships between dependent and independent variables may be complex and difficult to forecast.

- Data must be available over a long period of time; trend projection cannot be applied to new markets or technologies.

- Only quantifiable variables are suitable for extrapolation; nonquantifiable parameters are excluded.

- It is difficult to acquire accurate baseline data.

The ideal methodology to follow when formulating a market trend projection is outlined in Figure 7-4. The method is simple and allows building a credible basis for a market or sales forecast, providing more accurate trend projection.

Alternative forecasting methods using time series data are available. A number of methods depend on forecasting total sales, while some allow segmenting time series data into component parts. All component segments are predicted separately and individual component forecasts added to provide a total market or industry forecast. Accuracy is heightened when using this forecasting method because individual market segments are integrated into the overall market forecast.

Many sales and market forecasting methods are based on trend projection of volume (unit sales) or values (dollar sales). But projection is not limited to forecasting these variables. An alternative is to plot the previously observed market shares of market leaders and project any identified trend. It is extremely difficult to forecast market share and results often prove unreliable.

Figure 7-4
Building Forecast Material for Trend Projection

Determine Historical Trends

Historical trend information should provide historical data regarding price trends, historical sales, and market shares. To obtain this, you can:

- Conduct secondary research, by accumulating published information and industry reports; or

- Conduct primary research, by completing interviews with leading market competitors.

Quantify Base Year Numbers

You can also conduct interviews with the following groups to determine the accuracy of established base year numbers and projected trends.

- Producers

- End-users

- Government agencies

- Market research experts

The concept of market share is multidimensional — a market may be divided by total volume, total market value, geographic area, or other factors. Market share can be calculated for each of the segments and forecast on perceived trends. The basic steps for market share trend projection are:

- Define the objectives of the forecast.

- Identify market segments.

- Accumulate data for each market segment for the previous five years.

- Organize the data into a table.

- Identify trends and project data.

- Gather company sales data over the preceding five years.

- Compare company sales by product segment to total sales over the period to define market share data and past and projected trends.

- Convert projected market share values to unit sales and compare with unit sales projections to determine consistency.

The third basic market forecasting technique, the informal method, may be ideal for your business.

Informal forecasting methods involve developing and using models created for forecasting. Changes in the extent of commodity unit or dollar sales in the model occur in response to changes in one or more of the model's variables.

Informal Forecasting Methods

Several key methods are available to you, including:

- Casual regression models,
- Buyer intention surveys,
- Leading indicators,
- Input-output models, and
- Econometric models.

Read the following sections to learn what method might be best for your business.

Causal Regression Models. Informal forecasting methods require that you identify causal or predictor variables and then measure or estimate changes in these variables. These variables and other factors differ and can include relative prices and promotional expenditures. To develop a causal regression model, follow five key steps.

- Step 1 – Identify primary sales predictor variables. Variables must be measurable or easily quantifiable or both to be useful.
- Step 2 – Accumulate time series data on each predictor variable selected.
- Step 3 – Determine the relationship between each predictor variable and sales.
- Step 4 – Perform regression analysis to determine coefficients.
- Step 5 – Repeat the above steps until a suitable model is found. An effective model has the capability to accurately forecast historical data.

For example, as a result of following the above five steps, you may discover that portable computer purchasing is a function of two variables:

- Income
- Availability and cost of software

Buyer Intention Surveys. Surveys of buyer intentions use end-users to forecast their purchases in either units or dollar sales. Industrial and consumer product surveys are performed frequently in the United States and their accuracy varies widely. Forecasts for industrial products have been considerably more accurate than forecasts for consumer products.

As an astute analyst, you can then forecast changes in variables. Based on knowledge of the functional relationship between identified variables and portable computer purchases, you can generate a sales forecast.

Several surveys of projected business plant and equipment purchases are conducted in the United States. The most widely recognized surveys are conducted by McGraw-Hill Publishing, the Bureau of Economic Analysis, and the Conference Board.

Leading Indicators (Barometric Forecasting). Leading indicators, or barometric forecasting, are particularly useful to a company or industry producing products dependent on certain variables. Changes in these variables are used to anticipate changes in industry or company sales.

Leading indicators are primarily used to forecast fluctuations in the broader business environment as opposed to forecasting sales of individual companies or specific markets.

Specific problems associated with using leading indicators exist.

- The directions of economic movement pointed to by each group of leading indicators are rarely identical.

- Leading indicators can produce false signals. Leading indicators have a reasonably good track record in predicting turning points but occasionally predict turning points that do not occur.

The U.S. Department of Commerce gathers and publishes monthly data on 40 different time series that act as leading indicators to the direction of the overall U.S. economy. Data compiled by the U.S. Department of Commerce includes:

- New orders in durable goods industries;

- Industrial materials prices;

- Prices of 500 common stocks; and

- New business information.

Input-Output Models. The use of input-output (I-O) models is another method of casual or informal forecasting. When used for marketing industrial products, input-output analysis measures changes, ensures identification of the total potential market, and monitors the flow of business between supplying and user industries.

All U.S. companies maintain a ledger of their sales to other firms. If the ledgers for all companies competing in an industry were gathered and all data classified in terms of buyer and seller, the total sales made from selling to buying industries can be calculated.

Interindustry sales ledgers have been assembled for approximately 400 U.S. industries. The collected data is known as an input-output table and is basically a matrix of industry sales to itself and other industries.

Input-output tables have been used in forecasting to measure the overall economy as opposed to individual companies. These tables are predominantly used to determine the effects of changes in the amount of demand in one industry on others in the economy. Market forecasting using I-O tables is based on the premise that the output of a given industry is the predominant product input of another industry.

The principal advantages of input-output analysis as a forecasting tool are that it:

- Simplifies the relation of one segment forecast to another;

- Allows forecast accuracy cross-checks; and

- Simplifies segment forecasting, enhancing total market forecasts.

The principal disadvantages of input-output analysis are that it cannot account for:

- Effects of technological changes on interindustry sales;

- Changes in the product mix and the effects on interindustry sales;

- Changes in the role of government and the effects on interindustry sales; and

- Effects of changes in the relative prices of substitutes and components and the effects on interindustry sales.

Input-output analysis is often referred to as "top-down" forecasting. The market analysis begins by defining the total output then deriving the value of components or the input. Input is the dependent variable, output the independent variable.

The following factors demonstrate an effective method to acquire the base year input-output ratio.

- Input-output analysis is based on data acquired from product users, generally through interviews. The goal in interviewing is to determine the value ratio between the focus and the component products.

- The most effective way to achieve this goal is to determine total annual production of the output unit. This data can generally be acquired by interviewing the marketing department personnel of leading competitors.

- The value of purchases is determined by the input by interviewing purchasing department personnel.

- Once the values of output and input have been determined, compute the input-output ratio for the base year.

After determining your base year input-output ratio, determine anticipated ratio changes over the forecast period. Three variables to determine and project the trend are:

- Input product price trends,

- Output product price trends, and

- Trends in input quantity utilized per output.

Changes in input quantity are generally caused by technical changes and improvements in the input component. Product engineers can provide valuable information on projected technical improvements.

Price trend information can be based on historical information projected on the basis of perceived trends. Projected trend data should be supplemented by projections based on the estimates provided in interviews with industry marketing representatives.

Econometric Models. An econometric model is a system of interdependent simultaneous regression equations. As a result, their parameters must be estimated simultaneously. These models are generally used for forecasting macroeconomic conditions, such as gross national product (GNP) and investment.

Development of complex econometric models is often beyond the scope of a small company marketing group. Even in a large company environment the comprehensive statistical base required to make the model function realistically is often unavailable. Many large companies develop their own models for market and sales forecasting. The performance of econometric models in forecasting at the company and industry level remains undetermined.

Econometric models are increasingly used for informal forecasting. A considerable amount of economic literature in recent periods has focused on the development and description of alternative econometric models.

These models were initially developed to forecast the performance of entire economies. The first models appeared in the late 1950s. Comprehensive testing of econometric models began in the late 1960s and early 1970s. The results indicated that in terms of performance, no model was consistently superior to all others.

An easier trend analysis as outlined in earlier sections is suitable for routine sales and market forecasting.

General Comments

A number of market and sales forecasting methods have been outlined in this section. Use as many forecasting techniques as possible. Practical factors, such as time and cost constraints, need to be faced. It is unreasonable to assume that a single method of forecasting can be used alone for sales and market projection. Results obtained through different forecasting methods will vary. Comparing the results from different methods often illustrates a market growth or sales trend previously overlooked.

Forecasting Categories by Time Period

Long-, medium-, and short-term forecasts should always be distinguished. The terms long-, medium-, and short-term carry very different implications for different marketplaces and industries. For example, the short-term in the automobile industry is considerably longer than the short-term in the disposable medical products industry.

It is important to closely examine the nature of the market you forecast. Questions to consider include:

- What type of products does the industry manufacture?

- What is the comparative life cycle of the product and how does this impact the length of the forecast period?

Implications of selected forecast time periods on the structure and results of the forecast itself are significant. Because of the different time horizons of each forecasting method, the roles of long-, medium-, and short-term forecasting differ. Forecast use requirements differ by functional areas within the company organization.

The trend in business is to avoid medium- and long-term forecasting. The primary difficulty in all types of forecasting is anticipating where and when changes will occur. Minor short-term influences evolve into a significant trend in the medium- or long-term. To determine the full potential of trends, consider the long-term effects even when the immediate concern is short-term.

Short-Term Forecasts

The short-term period is any period long enough to permit variable production factors to be introduced in different combinations and amounts to maximize profits.

The short-term period is too brief to permit planning, purchasing, or bringing any piece of fixed capital — such as new plant and equipment — into operation.

The implications of short-term forecasts are many.

- Any short-term forecast may not exceed the existing capacity of the company or industry;

- Short-term demand is linked to and influenced by seasonal factors; and

- Seasonal demand, if in existence, can be linked to certain periods in most industries, making it possible to allow for peak periods in your forecasting.

If seasonal factors are relevant, adjust the short-term forecast seasonally instead of using a straight line trend.

The primary role of short-term forecasting during research is to determine the organization and scheduling of existing resources. The short-term forecast runs up to one year.

The status of existing variables is generally a reasonable indicator of near-term future behavior of the variable. Basic forecasting methods, such as time series analysis, can be used to generate accurate short-term forecasts.

The results of using short-term basic forecasting methods are often comparable to results obtained using more elaborate and complex forecasting methods. You can use short-term forecasting for:

- Production scheduling,

- Employment planning and distribution, and

- Market targeting and strategic planning.

If the short-term forecast is not right for your business, you may want to try a medium-term forecast.

Most industries readily acknowledge the existence of business cycles. Despite fluctuations, business patterns are characterized by stable cyclical movement.

Business cycle length varies among industries. In capital and industrial product industries a life cycle can extend from two to five years. Forecasting over periods of this length is more difficult than short-term forecasting. The principal difficulties arise in attempting to forecast changes in the business cycle.

Many companies use business cycles to forecast sales by adjusting factors influencing past sales and allowing for the impact of new influences in subsequent periods. Although it is possible to project declines or increases in sales, the magnitude of fluctuation is extremely difficult to predict.

Medium-term forecasts can be used for planning and formulating:

- Human resources budgets,

- Production budgets,

- Schedules, and

- Resource allocation for the production process.

Medium-term forecasts typically range from one to three years and are often constructed using several short-term forecasts. It is increasingly difficult for medium-term forecasts to anticipate vital changes either in overall economic activity or in a specific industry or market. The primary problems of medium-term forecasts are:

- Recessions, often completely unanticipated, can occur.

- Recessions or accelerations in economic activity are often extremely difficult to forecast.

- A multitude of available approaches for medium-term forecasting exists. Results can differ among forecasts.

If the medium-term forecast doesn't work, long-term forecasting may be the best alternative for your situation.

Long-term forecasts extend for three or more years. The goal of long-term forecasting is to provide an idea of likely market trends over a significant period of time. Accuracy is dependent upon events occurring in accordance with the assumptions made in the forecast. The long-range forecast illustrates overall movements within the industry. The market is not intended to be an exact representation of market sales for every year of a three- to twenty-year period.

Despite difficulties involved in constructing long-term forecasts, these forecasts play a vital role in modern business planning. Three principal roles of long-term forecasting exist.

- The longer the forecast time period, the greater the potential for unforeseen variables.

- The influence of broad economic factors begins to impact the forecasting process.

- Implications of demographic factors, trade cycles, international competition, income trends, and the development of new technologies must all be considered.

Long-term forecasts are frequently inaccurate and it is extremely difficult to assess the potential for forecast error. Unpredicted trend changes can occur as new events and conditions continually emerge. Historical data often provides an inaccurate picture of predominant trends. Difficulties involved in long-term forecasting include:

- Determining the long-term allocation of resources;

- Long-term planning of entry into new markets;

- Planning expansion of existing markets; and

- Product planning, development and diversification.

Long-term forecasts of 3 to 20 years should be considered trend data rather than highly detailed predictive forecasts. Long-term forecasts must consider factors other than recent market and sales data, such as:

- Long-term political indicators;

- National and international economic trends and factors; and

- Product life cycle.

General Comments

Market forecasts can be derived and projected using primary and secondary sources. The baseline database that you design provides the context for market growth estimates.

Historical data is often useful in forming baseline figures to provide a starting point for your forecast. Trending of historical figures can provide a fairly good picture of potential future growth trends.

Interviews with vendors and end-users are an excellent source of information for developing market growth forecasts and estimating development of significant trends. Figure 7-5 summarizes short-, medium-, and long-term forecasting and potential uses of interview data to assist in building your forecasts.

Forecasting Technological Trends

Technology forecasting is not concerned with precise and accurate projections of technological development. The goal of technological forecasting is to anticipate general trends. For example, it is extremely valuable for an aircraft design company to anticipate the types of aircraft design that will be predominant in 30 years. Technological forecasting can provide the company with some predictions of likely trends in aircraft design, but cannot predict the exact specifications of designs most likely to be favored in 30 years.

Forecasting technology contrasts with quantitative forecasting methodologies. Technology forecasting is a form of qualitative forecasting.

Figure 7-5
Short-, Medium-, and Long-Term Forecasts
and Potential Interview Data

Short-term (0-1 year). Vendors' opinions will be most credible, especially for their own companies. Vendors generally have a high level of knowledge for this time period.

Medium-term (1-3 years). Individual vendor opinions may not reflect consensus market opinion on emerging trends or future events. Aggregating vendor expectations for important trends may yield accurate estimates for this period.

Long-term (3+ years). Vendors generally have less information, and their opinions are often optimistic or less credible. In estimating long-term market demand, focus on significant future events with the potential to affect demand. These events may be economic, social, legislative, or demographic. Examples are the exhaustion of a computer architectural technology, the expiration of a product patent, or specific actions by market leaders.

Quantitative forecasting methods are generally employed for forecasting market dollar sales, commodity unit sales, growth rates, and other related business indicators.

When forecasting technology, do not rely on the extrapolation and projection of historical data patterns. Although historical information can play a role in forecasting technology, a constant projection of a past pattern into the future cannot be assumed.

Technological forecasting methodologies generally do not provide a detailed method of analysis. Numerical values are not usually provided.

To effectively use any technological forecasting method you must know the factors involved and have the capability to modify the forecast method to meet the requirements of the existing situation.

It is an increasing trend among U.S. companies to attempt to forecast technological development. The primary reasons underlying this trend are:

- To account for the effects of technology development on new product development;

- To allow for the impact of technological developments on the market forecast;

- For industry innovators to maintain their leadership, they must forecast technological trends; and

- Companies following the leads set by industry innovators require a working knowledge of the potential technological directions of the market.

All firms competing in markets where technology is a key differentiator can benefit from technology forecasting.

All technology forecasting methods fall into two distinct categories: exploratory techniques and normative techniques.

Exploratory forecasting uses existing information regarding the potential of science and prevailing technical trends and does not account for other structural changes that may impact the assumed trend.

Normative forecasting functions in reverse, starting in the future and working backward to the present. Normative technological forecasting attempts to predict future technological needs and requirements. Technology goals, objectives, and the technological developments necessary to achieve them can then be calculated.

The Economic Environment

When forecasting sales, market growth, or technological development, consider the underlying trends in the overall economic environment. Fluctuations in the extent of economic activity can have a significant effect on market and technological development trends. Any forecast neglecting to reference trends in the economic environment is likely to be inaccurate.

A good starting point for any market or sales forecast for particular product groups is to use an indicator pertaining to the total economy. Trends anticipated for the overall economy can have a marked effect on your product forecast, particularly if you are using some form of trend extrapolation as a forecast method.

Economic indicators reference an extremely wide range of financial and economic data providing a clear picture of movement in various segments of the economy. By following the direction of the overall economic trends pointed to by the indicators, you can put your own forecasting in perspective by negating any excessive optimism or pessimism.

The overall impact of the economic environment is not limited to market and sales forecasting. Technology forecasts can also be impacted by trends in the economy. Market forces often reinforce and encourage technical trends.

Technological development in a specific area is likely to be accelerated if a significant market application for the technology is expected. Expected extensive use of the technology and profits generated by that use are likely to encourage investment.

Added investment can lead to heightened research and development expenditure and the likely acceleration of technological development. Market forces and technological development must go hand-in-hand.

Certain market forces will encourage rapid development of a particular technology. Market forces will likely encourage development of a new technology if:

- The product offers improved cost-effectiveness;

- The technology expands potential applications; or

- The technology is supplied by a number of market competitors. (The existence of competition encourages rapid technical development.)

Other market forces have the potential to provide a disincentive to the development of a particular technology. Low levels of promotion for a certain technology often result in poor market performance, as will low levels of end-user education offered by the originators of the technology.

Notes

Chapter 8

Market Analysis Techniques

Eight major market analysis techniques are outlined in this chapter, including:

- Sales analysis,

- Saturation rates,

- Price analysis,

- Market share analysis,

- Product life cycles,

- New technological trends,

- Risk assessment, and

- Sales potential.

Generally, no one market analysis technique is consistently superior to all others — the ideal approach is to use a combination of methods.

An analysis of a marketplace using separate analytical techniques allows comparison of the results of different techniques, providing a number of insights regarding the workings of the marketplace.

Sales Analysis

To the competent market researcher, the simple company sales invoice is a potentially valuable source of market information. The sales invoice can tell where the particular end-user is located, the products purchased, total units shipped, and shipment dates. Data concerning sales representative performance and particular sales territories can also be acquired through sales invoices.

Information derived from sales analysis may be combined with other market and product data to provide information on sales by:

- Product
- End-user
- Geographic region
- Salesperson
- Sales territory

Sales performance is an essential component in the performance evaluation of any company. Sales analysis allows you to set sales targets for sales regions, territories, and representatives. Subsequent sales evaluation determines how well targets have been met.

Sales analysis and forecasting are different from market research and forecasting. Typically, sales analysis and forecasting focus on the short-term, with forecasting based primarily on trend projection.

Sales analysis and forecasting are oriented toward supporting the sales function — determining how well the sales group is performing, examining if any means are available to improve performance, and forecasting performance quarterly, semiannually, and yearly. While sales analysis differs from market research, the information base necessary to maintain a market research group can contribute significantly to sales analysis.

Saturation Rates

Saturation rates pertain to a product life cycle. The various stages of this life cycle are essential if you are to link marketing dynamics to your forecast.

Each stage of the life cycle can be identified by certain characteristics of the level of sales. Ideal courses of action and market strategies are appropriate to each stage of the product life cycle.

The rate of saturation is the rate at which the product reaches the saturation stage of its life cycle. Figure 8-1 helps identify the life cycle process and the effect of the saturation stage on sales.

The saturation stage is characterized by intense market competition and considerable sales promotion. During this stage, manufacturers attempt to expand their share of the market at the expense of their competitors. Typical market competitor response includes:

- Cutting expenditures;
- Defending existing market share;
- Attempting to offer lower prices; and
- Attempting to find ways to differentiate products without adding to production costs.

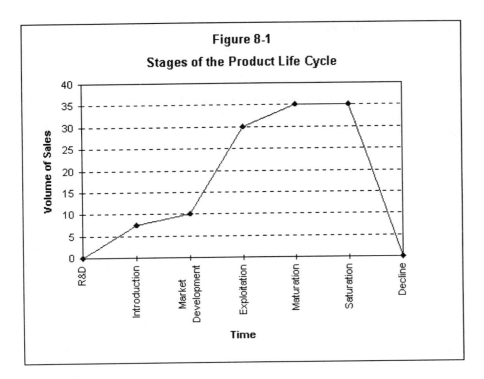

Figure 8-1

Stages of the Product Life Cycle

During the initial segment of the saturation stage, price competition is typically intense as manufacturers force down their costs and take advantage of economies of scale.

As the saturation stage continues, the structure of the industry typically begins to change. The number of competitors drops and products become increasingly standardized, allowing for further development of economies of scale.

With the onset of the saturation period, the marketing mix of competitors should change to reflect a product in the latter stages of its life cycle. The long-term success of the company will depend on the effect of the marketing mix the company adopts. The typical features of the saturation stage include:

- Low sales growth;
- Falling profits;
- Minimal technical product differentiation;
- Intense competition, increased takeover activity;
- Stable prices; and
- Few market entrants.

By plotting and monitoring sales, it is possible for you to monitor the product life cycle to determine the rate of saturation. Market strategy can be effectively prepared to deal with rapidly changing market conditions and intensifying competition when the life cycle reaches the maturation-saturation stage.

The impending saturation stage is characterized by a leveling of the sales growth experienced during the market development and exploitation stages of the life cycle.

Price Analysis

Product pricing decisions are an essential component of overall market strategy. An analysis of your prices in the marketplace can reveal a great deal about the reasons behind your product performance in particular market segments.

The way you price a product has a substantial effect on the commodity units purchased by end-users. Changes in price levels can cause changes in demand for a product.

The goal of price analysis is to assist in the development of a pricing plan. The plan should indicate appropriate price levels to use when introducing a new product and the price levels most appropriate during subsequent stages of the product life cycle.

The impact of any planned changes in product price should always be considered when putting together market and sales forecasts.

Decisions regarding appropriate product price ranges should always be made in the early stages of product development. Decisions concerning the final product price levels should be made just before product introduction. Three forms of product pricing strategy are widely used.

- Pricing strategies seeking to maximize market share. When this strategy is adopted, your business enters the market at the lowest price possible. Prices are continually lowered as heightened volume sales bring down production costs.

- Pricing strategies seeking to maximize profits. This strategy attempts to maximize attainable profits in each sales period.

- Market information required for each type of pricing strategy differs widely. The information is used to differentiate between types of analyses used in the two approaches.

To maximize market share, adjust prices by following these five steps.

- Step 1 – Define the experience curve.
- Step 2 – Calculate break-even points.
- Step 3 – Define unit costs for units sold into additional market segments.
- Step 4 – Determine competitor costs.
- Step 5 – Forecast the product life cycle through to the decline stage.

Businesses that use profit maximization as a pricing strategy attempt to price their product at the point where profits will be most significant until shifts in market conditions dictate price changes. When this strategy is used, the appropriate price encourages a significant difference between cost and revenues.

As a research analyst, your role is to forecast cost and revenues over a series of relevant prices. Several methods exist for forecasting units sold relative to the unit prices set. Primary forecasting methods for forecasting units sold relative to prices set include:

- Judgmental forecasting (the Delphi method);
- Statistical analysis of sales information;
- Sales testing; and
- Laboratory tests and simulation.

Judgmental forecasting and sales and lab testing methods are described in Chapter 7. Statistical sales data analysis is useful in separating the effects of price on quantities sold as opposed to the effects of other variables.

Regression analysis is the most widely used method. Records are regularly updated to ensure that the inferences you draw regarding the effects of prices on past sales are reasonable. Further, you should keep a record of significant marketing activities in each sales territory or region. You can monitor:

- The pricing strategy of your competitors — movements in competitor prices over time;
- Increased competitor promotion and advertising activity;
- New product releases;
- Expansion of competitor sales facilities; and
- Changes in the capacity of your production facility (such as plants closing or strikes).

Keeping a record of significant historical events impacting the marketing function allows more accurate interpretation of historical sales information to identify the total effects of pricing strategy. The record should note the time and nature of events to assess their impact on sales records.

Market Share Analysis

Market share means the percentage of market commodity unit volume or dollar value held by a company. Most firms are concerned with their share of actual markets as opposed to potential markets.

Attaining the highest market share possible is a desirable objective. Generally, regardless of your product's price, you will remain comparatively more profitable than your competitors if you have a higher market share. You must ensure that your market is clearly defined. The underlying reason for small companies functioning profitably in large marketplaces is that they have developed a large share of a small subsegment of the total market.

Keep in mind, one of the ultimate goals of any business is to encourage growth of its market share. It is expensive and difficult to increase market share in slowly growing markets. A small number of competitors generally dominate markets in the saturation stage of their life cycle.

In markets characterized by high growth, your goal is to develop market share by obtaining a larger percentage than the competition. In an attempt to save money, a number of businesses have adopted the complacent attitude of merely trying to maintain their current share. Businesses that adopt this approach are actually losing share to the competition.

Market share analysis and forecasting may be most simply performed by plotting historical market share information and projecting future trends. Market share trend projection can reveal aspects of the market not clarified in other market variable projections.

A Multidimensional Concept

The concept of market share is multidimensional. The first step is to define all market segments and determine your company's share of each. As you calculate and forecast each segment of the markets in which you compete, you learn about factors impacting market share. The unclaimed share in each forecast represents your competitors' share. Projecting their shares is an excellent way to supplement your competitive analysis.

When forecasting your market share remember that, regardless of market size in units or dollars, combined market shares must equal 100 percent. After projecting your shares and those of your competitors, compare the market share forecast to forecasts for the market or product group to ensure consistency. Use the following key steps when forecasting your competitors' market share:

- Determine the objectives of the analysis. Decide on which market segments to focus.

- Determine methods to use for analysis and projection.

- Gather historical market sales data for the relevant market segments for the preceding five-year period.

- Arrange the data in tables and plot the historical information.

- Project the market sales into the future based on the historical trend. Use your judgment and market segment experience when forming the forecast.

- Gather company-specific market segment sales data for the same five-year period and compare company-specific sales per period to total sales at the time to determine market shares. Use your judgment, knowledge, and experience to help form the forecasts.

- Reconvert calculated market shares to dollar and unit values and make consistency comparisons. Combine market share forecasts for various market segments the company competes in to provide an impression of your overall market share.

Estimating your competitors' current market share is not an easy task — this information is generally proprietary and companies attempt to conceal it. Likely sources of competitor market share information by product line are:

- 10K annual reports (if the company is publicly owned);

- Interviews with counterparts at competing firms;

- Interviews with significant end-users; and

- Lost business reports submitted by your company's salespeople.

Market share information should be accumulated and the trend information used as input in the decision making process. As time passes, your actual market share performance should be compared against actual share performance.

Comparing your competitor's share performance and examining their market strategies may help in formulating invaluable plans for changes in your own strategies. A perception of competitors' market share positions can help predict future patterns in their behavior and their potential reactions to the competitive behavior of your company.

A working knowledge of market share and the extent of market penetration is essential for the necessary allocation of resources for the sales department. The potential benefits of detailed analysis in this area are limitless.

Product Life Cycles

The product life cycle describes the sales pattern of a product over time. Generally, the time span commences with product introduction and concludes with its obsolescence and replacement. Marketing strategies need to be modified as the product passes through each stage of the cycle.

While the form of the life cycle is basically standard, it is subject to variations. The premise of the product life cycle is that all products pass through specific phases when they are on the market. The basic product life cycle is extremely effective in forecasting the pattern of sales growth for a product in the market. The basic life cycle concept suggests that all products pass through four stages:

- Development

- Growth

- Maturity

- Decline

This concept is shown in Figure 8-2.

The first of the four stages represents slow growth periods. It is assumed that new products require some time to gain market acceptance so sales in the initial period are slow.

If the product introduction proves successful, rapid growth stages are reached and sales increase markedly. According to the concept of the life cycle, the market for any product is limited and sales will generally fall short of their full potential. When this point is reached, the market enters its maturation stage. The life cycle also assumes that each product is eventually replaced by another or that initial rapid growth will end in decline.

If a product enters a mature market, competition is intense as the product competes for a share of an existing market currently not experiencing growth.

Once the market enters the decline stage, new products are not entering the market and demand levels are falling. At this point the objective is to increase market share to maintain sales levels.

The Key to Forecasting

The concept of the product life cycle has become central to market forecasting. The stages of the life cycle form a framework for analyzing the dynamics and primary factors impacting market segment and product sales. The product life cycle is primarily used to:

- Clearly delineate the relationship between profits and sales; and

- Provide a planning and forecasting time benchmark. This adds an air of reality to the forecast not available when accounting time units are arbitrarily employed.

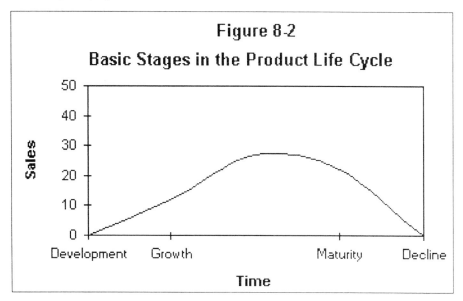

The life cycle concept or curve can be approached in two ways. A potential curve uses an analysis of underlying market factors to build the curve. A realized curve is the end result of your marketing strategy to impact factors underlying the market.

The basic stages of the product life cycle can be expanded to better explain various subsegments of the life of a product in the market. The various stages of the expanded product life cycle concept include:

- Research and development,

- Product introduction,

- Market development,

- Exploitation,

- Market maturation,

- Market saturation, and

- Market decline.

The implications of the product life cycle as a planning and forecasting tool are many and varied. It is vital for the marketing function that both sales and profits be planned over the entire expected product life. Profits are the key to the continued existence of your business, so forecasting and planning of this variable are vital.

Profits are nonexistent during the research and development stage. In rare circumstances, profits are made early in the life cycle. Generally, profits are not made until the development of the market stage, particularly in highly competitive markets; at this point, products not having reached profitability are usually withdrawn from the market.

Profits reach their zenith during the exploitation stage. Maturation and saturation stages are characterized by steady to declining profits, usually due to increased competition. Profits continue to decline to the point where they no longer exist and losses take hold during the product decline stage.

The life cycle is vital as a planning unit because of the extent of profit shifts during each stage of the cycle. Forecasting and planning over the medium-term can be effective when using the product life cycle segments as timing stage.

The product life cycle can also be used to help determine likely future competitive trends. There are six typical levels of competition for each stage of the production process.

- Product introduction — Levels of competition are practically nonexistent as the company introducing the product is the sole supplier.

- Market development — The market is still dominated by the product innovator. Other companies have entered the market and developed smaller shares.

- Exploitation stage — A single company remains the primary force in the market although it may not be the product originator. The product innovator may have been overtaken by subsequent market entrants. The market leader may be fending off leadership challenges from other large competitors. Generally, the leading company's share will experience decline over this period as competitive activity in the market continues.

- Maturation stage — The leading company usually maintains its leadership position, but its share is smaller than the combined share of all other market competitors.

- Saturation stage — The major market share is dominated by product types other than that of the market leader. Smaller competitors are trying to secure a market niche that they can dominate. Toward the conclusion of the saturation period, three or four competitors typically emerge to

Plan for Profit

dominate the market. Vigorous marketing allows these competitors to hold the majority share.

■   Decline stage — The market leader during the saturation stage may be replaced by a competitor better suited to competing in small, contracting markets. As specialized market segments continue to decline in scale, large-scale producers cease to perceive them as profitable. Shares typically diminish across the board as products become more generic.

Recognizing the current stage of the product life cycle is vital to introducing a new product. It is considerably easier to enter a market in a growth stage than to enter a saturated, mature marketplace.

Levels of competition in markets experiencing growth are considerably less intense than in mature markets where competitors are more concerned about loss of sales and market share. Introducing a product into an intensely competitive market is usually expensive and results in retaliation from established competitors.

The primary reason for stressing the importance of product life cycles is that each stage of the product life cycle uses a marketing strategy appropriate to the unique demands of the situation.

Market factors, such as supply and demand, change constantly as they pertain to the company, market, and industry. A detailed knowledge of appropriate product life cycles can make market strategy more timely and effective.

New Technological Trends

Technological development is not an independent variable — certain forces drive development, others retard it. Any analysis of a new technological trend should consider both. A comprehensive understanding of the existing and potential behavior of these forces, although difficult to achieve, makes it possible to construct an overview of the potential for development of new technology.

Changes in technology significantly affect the development of future marketplaces so analysis of new technology and market analysis cannot be segregated. Because a technology is more likely to develop rapidly if an existing product application is available, developing a technology and a market for that technology are mutually reinforcing activities. New technology results in profits and market development — the expected viability of a technology is instrumental in generating investment and rapid growth. The potential driving factors include:

■   Economic rewards,

■   Strong, well-developed research group,

■   Heavy financial support, and

■   Heavy management backing.

The potential retarding factors include:

■   No apparent economic reward,

- Numerous established competing technologies,

- No practical applications, and

- Numerous existing physical limitations.

Undertaking any new activity in unfamiliar territory involves considerable risk. Your business may undertake risk by advancing into one of these areas, or increase risk by simultaneously entering more than one. A high degree of risk is associated with:

Risk Assessment

- Entry into new markets;

- Introduction of new products; and

- Development of new technologies.

You incur the maximum degree of risk when a new product based on a new technology enters a new market. Usually, companies undertake this risk because the returns are enormous, if the ploy is successful.

Market research allows you to convert uncertainty to calculated risk and provides data to help minimize these risks. Accurate market research and analysis can help uncover potential new markets and assist in identifying existing entry barriers. Timely market information and accurate forecasting can prove vital in determining risk levels associated with development of a new product.

Uncertainty arises when outcomes are considered equally possible. Assigning probabilities to particular outcomes converts them to a risk — a quantified uncertainty. If you assign probabilities to certain events occurring in response to your decisions, decision making improves and you operate under conditions of calculated risk as opposed to complete uncertainty.

There is a growing propensity to use acquisition as the key to expansion into high risk areas. Numerous companies have jumped into completely unrelated areas of operation by acquiring other companies. Since the result of these acquisitions are generally below expectations, management increasingly targets companies having interests common to their own.

Sales Potential

If calculated carefully, comparing increases and decreases in actual sales against potential sales can prove a valuable indicator of company performance. You can use sales potential estimates for:

- Formulating marketing budgets;

- Company performance evaluations; and

- Identifying sales targets.

Estimates of sales potential and potential sales are not identical. Sales potential indicates sales capable of being developed but not presently existing — sales that would arise if the market were fully developed.

Several methods for estimating sales potential are available. Primary methods include:

- End-user surveys,
- Purchase proportion,
- Correlative indexes, and
- Adjusted industry sales.

Purchase proportion is often used to estimate total sales potential for specific territories when industry sales data is unavailable. In these cases, industry sales are estimated and the figure adjusted to obtain sales potential estimates.

Correlative indexes are used to determine the relative market potential of different geographic territories. The calculation assumes that when one series demonstrates a significant degree of correlation to another, the first may be used to estimate the second.

Adjusted industry sales are statistics compiled by trade associations, and government and other agencies. Sales potential estimates are indicative of sales that can be achieved as opposed to actual sales. Industry sales estimates should be used as a base and appropriate adjustments made to determine total sales potential.

An Optimal Integration of Techniques

Each analysis method provides information on gaining valuable insight into different aspects of the marketplace. To get an accurate picture of all facets of the market, use as many analytical techniques as possible. Some integration of analysis methods generally provides the best results.

Chapter 9

Setting Up a Market Information System (MIS)

Today, more businesses are monitoring their markets for changes rather than correcting problems after they have occurred. This type of proactive approach calls for a market information system (MIS) — a series of procedures and methods organized for the regular, planned collection, analysis, and presentation of information used in the marketing decision making process.

The key word in the above definition is regular. The emphasis in market research is on establishing systems that generate data for the marketing decision making process on a regular basis, as opposed to conducting research efforts as the need arises.

Market research is the systematic recording, gathering, and analysis of data related to the movement of goods and services. The difference between market research and the MIS is slight — both have identical objectives, but the differentiating factor is the regularity of information flows.

Plans can only be as effective as the information upon which they are based. Without accurate, up-to-the-minute information, it is extremely difficult to rationally plan for your business.

The most significant difficulty of the research procedure has been its irregularity. Research projects are often undertaken on a crisis basis. Information is gathered in lumps and analyzed in large quantities over a brief period in an attempt to solve problems as they arise. The intelligent management approach realizes that rational decision making requires a continuous flow of information input.

Defining a Market Information System (MIS)

How a Market Information System Functions

The objective of the MIS is to maintain business activity at an optimal level. This is accomplished by constantly monitoring business activity via the MIS. The MIS sends signals to management of unwanted fluctuation in a variable monitored by the system, providing an information basis to rectify the problem.

Variables, such as profits, sales, installed base, and market share, are closely monitored to ensure adequate control.

Design Considerations when Organizing the MIS

A multitude of alternatives are available to anyone contemplating the development of an MIS. You should consider several key factors, including:

- Parameters to monitor, such as market share, exports, market size, and pricing,
- Data sources,
- Data currency,
- Aggregation of data,
- Sophistication of analysis,
- Data storage considerations, and
- Reporting of data.

Data Currency

Data currency refers to the time between event occurrence and entering of the event into the MIS. Movements in variables monitored by the MIS can be entered into the data as they occur, or at the end of the day, week, or month.

The MIS is operating in real time if sales, inventory, or purchasing data are entered as changes occur. The use of remote computer terminals permits acquisition of up-to-the-minute data to assist specific management decisions. The system is only as accurate and timely as the data.

The impact of data currency depends on how the data is used. In some industries the need for immediate data is minimal; while in others it can make the difference between the success or failure of the marketing decision.

Aggregation of Data

Aggregation of data refers to the accuracy of the data entered into the system. Sales data may be entered individually, complete with customer identification codes, or the data may be aggregated with other sales information to compile broader indicators of sales by representative region.

Data can be entered in a variety of different methods. The method of data aggregation or disaggregation you select can seriously affect the MIS design.

Analytical Sophistication

Analytical sophistication refers to the complexity of models incorporated into the market information system. If computers are used in the MIS, low analytical sophistication levels will require the computer to recognize and retrieve certain records. High levels of sophistication will require the computer to use existing data to provide indicators of future occurrences.

While it is not necessary to use a computer in the management information system, the role of the computer refers to the degree of decision making capacity delegated to a computer by management.

Data Storage

A computer may be integrated into an MIS to inform management when sales inventory falls below a certain level or programmed to issue a directive for ordering more inventory.

The key role of the computer today can be in database management systems. A considerable level of detail goes into the data collection and entry process. A computer can quickly sort out many significant trends that typically cannot be observed through manual data manipulation.

The elements involved in the overall design framework of the MIS are vital in determining the future value of the system. The design process must be systematic.

Essential Factors in Determining MIS Design

System design is essential because the MIS structures interaction between people, equipment, and processes to provide a relevant flow of information from both internal and external sources. The information sequence is important because it forms the basis of decisions in specified management areas.

Decision making plays an integral role in marketing. The time and resources allocated to information flow organization represent an essential investment. Research indicates that the market intelligence system generally remains one of the most inefficiently organized areas of management. In fact, the disappointing impact of computers in improving MIS design is attributed to the poor initial design framework of the majority of systems.

The inability to formulate a clear definition of the market information required as MIS input is the primary factor causing poor design and organization of the MIS. Executives commonly fail to pinpoint key indicators of success such as market share, the necessity for follow-up service, and other important factors. As a result, large volumes of useless or unnecessary data are often produced because management has failed to clearly identify its information requirements.

Four steps should be followed in determining MIS information requirements.

All existing information and data available within your company must be assembled. The list should include:

Step 1 — Assemble a Detailed List

- Sales figures by product, customer, location, price, amount, and date;
- End-user data;
- Competitor product literature;
- Product development data;
- Inventory data;
- Competitor profile data;
- Advertising information;
- Export/import data;

- Economic data; and

- Competitor data, such as pricing and commodity unit sales estimates.

Step 2 — Understand Each Manager's Role

Each manager should list all decisions he or she regularly makes in addition to the data routinely required to make those decisions. To achieve this, an objective assessment of each manager's decision making responsibilities and capabilities must be made. Consider the following questions:

- What sort of decisions is each decision maker regularly called to make?

- What forms of data are required to make these decisions?

- What types of studies are regularly requested?

- What additional data would the decision makers like to receive?

- Which information should be received in daily, weekly, monthly, and annual intervals?

- Which trade journals and magazines should be received on a regular basis?

- If an MIS is already in operation, are there any improvements the decision maker would like to see?

Step 3 — Know What Data You Need

Decisions regularly made must be logically combined with the data required to make these decisions. An example is shown below:

Decision: Desirable new product features

Data: End-user opinions regarding the existing product

Generally, a variety of redundancies in information requirements appear. Potential combinations of data and management decision can be placed in a matrix. All combinations can then be examined and potential purpose noted. A regularly produced product line report should provide the decision maker with the varying performance of product lines within certain geographic areas.

Step 4 — Organize the MIS Structure

The final step in the process is the most difficult and involves organizing the MIS structure. Once the previous steps are worked through in detail, the information requirements of the system will be determined. System designers must then evaluate costs and organizational structure.

Figure 9-1 displays a typical MIS structure.

The Building Block Approach

It is not wise to initially attempt a fully integrated MIS. The ideal course is to adopt a building block approach. Each block in the system represents a self-contained subsystem meeting a discrete management information requirement. A more integrated system that operates in line with the needs and experience of end-users is developed as discrete blocks are added to the system.

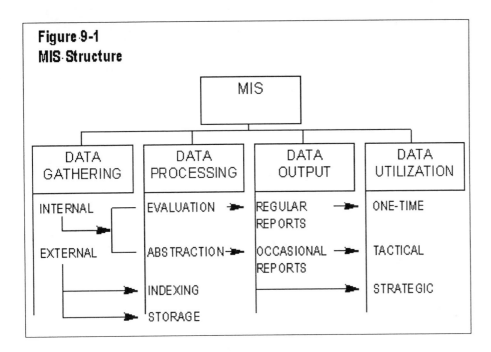

Figure 9-1
MIS Structure

Two alternatives for information collection and storage exist — information may be aggregated or disaggregated. Aggregated collection and data storage entails the gathering and grouping of related data in one file with no segregation of related information. An aggregated end-user file can place end-user names, financial records, and transaction records without segregation. A disaggregated data file system will store data in a segregated manner. End-user files are comprised of a series of files with all of the above mentioned data stored by category.

The advantages of disaggregated collection and storage of information are numerous. However, maintenance of disaggregated data often becomes expensive and management must weigh the additional benefits against potential costs. The primary drawback of aggregating information is that potential changes in the state of the market may necessitate broad-based modification of the MIS not easily achieved with aggregated data.

The flowchart shown in Figure 9-1 is a comparatively simple model of one possible MIS structure. Once the information requirements of the MIS have been calculated, the organization of an appropriate MIS information flow structure is essential. To begin, have a basic idea of the fundamentals of structuring MIS organization. To do this,

- List your company's decision making information requirements;

- Consider and list the resources (workforce and material) at hand for data gathering, processing, and output; and

- List ways to organize the resources to effectively meet existing requirements.

Although they are not required, personal or mainframe computers are extremely useful in MIS organizing.

**Aggregated Versus
Disaggregated Data**

A Proven MIS Method

Your business can use an easy method to organize its MIS structure. This simple method involves three key phases, including:

- Data gathering,
- Data processing, and
- Data output and use.

Data Gathering

Organize an individual or group of researchers to assemble all available information into required categories. Segregate the data into internal and external information. Competitor data may consist of internally generated estimates and some external information in the form of an annual report. Data comes in a number of forms and may include annual reports, internal sales and inventory records, competitor product literature, end-user surveys, end-user complaints, suggestions, and transaction records.

It is useful to separate internal and external information during the data gathering stage, as this information will subsequently be processed, output, and used in different ways.

Data Processing

The research individual or group now processes the information. Internal and external data should be processed separately.

Internally generated data must be critically evaluated to avoid redundancies. Redundant or unwanted information should be discarded to avoid large quantities of unnecessary data.

After the evaluation stage, internal data should be abstracted by the researcher. Often a large document contains only a single page of essential information. Abstracting internal data and isolating key information points will save considerable time and effort in the long-run.

External data should be indexed and stored for potential use. If a computer is not available, start with a filing cabinet to index and store internal and external data separately. Use disaggregated data files. Examples of information included in a disaggregated end-user file are:

- End-user company name,
- Type of business,
- End-user address,
- End-user financial records,
- Chronological listing of transactions, and
- Product application.

MIS files should be carefully structured and indexed in a logical format so data can be easily accessed. If telephone surveys are a part of the external data gathering process, tape recordings and written transcripts of the telephone interviews should be made and appropriately stored.

Data Output and Use

MIS data input varies with the purpose of decision makers. Internal data is generally available in the form of regular or occasional reports. Regular reports are used periodically for decision making on a single basis. Occasional reports are required by marketing decision makers for tactical decisions on a more infrequent basis.

External data is generally used on a limited basis when special data is requested by marketing decision makers for strategic decisions. The data often consists of telephone and mail surveys specifically conducted for strategic decision making. Often this data will be in the form of specially requested reports containing survey results and other research findings.

Five Misconceptions Regarding the Role of the MIS

An effective way to illustrate critical factors in MIS design is to explain some of the most frequent misconceptions on system design. The most prevalent of these misconceptions are that:

- More data is needed;
- Management's conceptions of necessary data;
- Data will result in improved decision making;
- Enhanced communication leads to enhanced performance; and
- Management understanding of the MIS function is not necessary.

Misconception 1 – The Need for More Relevant Data

The majority of MISs are designed with the misconception that most managers lack relevant data. While it is true that many managers suffer this problem, a more important difficulty is an oversupply of irrelevant data.

The MIS should eliminate irrelevant data as well as supply relevant data. The MIS has become both a quality filter and a data consolidator.

Misconception 2 – Managers' Conceptions of Necessary Data

A standard procedure for designing an MIS is to ask managers and decision makers what type of data they would like the system to provide. This is based on the misconception that managers are totally aware of the data they require.

To be aware of all information needed, managers must know all the decisions they make and have a developed model of each one. Unfortunately, this rarely occurs.

To adequately specify data requirements, a model of each decision process must be developed by categorizing variables. Information systems cannot be adequately designed unless the control system is taken into account because information systems are integral components of control systems.

Misconception 3 – Data Will Result in Improved Decision Making

It is often assumed by MIS designers that if management is provided with the required data, decision making will improve. Even when a manager is provided with the required data, he or she may have difficulty using it to optimum efficiency. The ability of managers to use certain data should therefore be assessed before system design.

If the decision making process is complex, it often becomes difficult for a manager to use market data. Rules and guidelines for data use should be provided by MIS system designers and managers should receive performance feedback assessing their ability to use data produced by the MIS.

Misconception 4 – Enhanced Communication Leads to Enhanced Performance

MISs often provide managers with improved indications of what managers in other divisions or departments are doing. MIS designers assume that improved intercompany communications will enhance a company's overall performance. This is not always the case. Measures of performance often differ between departments, so communication between groups may create confusion and hinder the organization rather than help it.

Misconception 5 – Management's Understanding of the MIS Function

MIS designers frequently provide a manager with easy methods of accessing MIS data and assure the manager that he or she need not know anything more about how the system functions. This leaves management unable to assess MIS performance. A significant proportion of MIS control is delegated to system designers or trained controllers who have no understanding of management requirements.

MISs should not be used unless the management that the system is designed to support fully comprehends how to control and evaluate system performance.

The Reality of the MIS

The MIS may be divided into two integral systems: operating systems and support systems. The operating system integrates all procedures used by managers in making their marketing decisions.

An efficient management system should provide management with the data necessary to adequately perform its duties. The form the MIS data takes is not specified by the operating system; the data may be presented in a number of formats, such as a typed document or a computer printout.

The support system incorporates all activities necessary to generate the report, such as data acquisition, storage retrieval, and transmission. Market research groups and data processing are considered support groups.

Regardless of how carefully an MIS is designed, it is unlikely that the system will anticipate all future information requirements of management. Situations change rapidly with the introduction of new products, expansion of sales territories, and changes in company organization. Thus, two additional factors should be included in system design: adaptability and flexibility.

MIS Must Be Adaptable and Flexible

The system must be adaptable to allow for new information and changes in decision making styles. Fluctuations in these parameters may require information design changes in the system. Thus, the MIS must be flexible. One key feature of an MIS is that it provides the tools or channels for new information needs. Should new demands for information suddenly arise, they can be quickly satisfied if the company is using an MIS.

To ensure MIS adaptability, the system should set up using disaggregated data files. The cornerstone of a successful system should be a subsystem of disaggregated data files.

A disaggregated data file makes it possible for your company to recreate dealings with customers over time. This type of file organization can be translated to all aspects of the company's activities. For example, disaggregated product files can be structured to provide a detailed listing of chronological sales for a particular product.

An MIS using a subsystem of disaggregated data files can evolve over time. If you have access to specific chronological information, you can test new concepts against historical information. If MIS data is placed in aggregate files, system modification is precluded; so the value of the system over time becomes questionable.

The primary impact of the MIS is in costs, sales analysis, and other functions commonly focused on by the marketing group. These activities are structured, well-defined, and permit easy reorganization of the MIS function. Most managers have been unwilling to allow computers to report on anything other than results deviating from the norm.

Impact of the MIS

An effective MIS system can reveal problems of which you have been completely unaware, including:

- Low sales in market subsegments;

- Highly competitive, previously insignificant sales in certain markets;

- Pricing strategy problems in certain markets; and

- Sales force territory allocation problems.

Figure 9-2 details the types of information an MIS can collect and transmit.

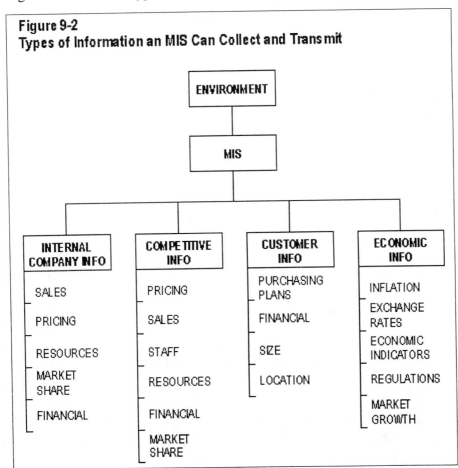

Figure 9-2
Types of Information an MIS Can Collect and Transmit

MIS Design Budgeting Considerations

To construct an MIS, market information must be produced, processed, stored, and distributed rapidly, because market research has a limited life span.

The value of market information is proportional — the less you know about a particular marketing problem, the more significant is the risk associated with an incorrect decision and the more valuable the market information becomes. The value of an MIS may be established through a cost/benefit appraisal of market information.

Weigh the Costs and Benefits

Costs are usually simple to identify. The benefits of an ordered, regular flow of market information are more difficult to establish. Benefits may be expressed by added profits arising through identification of market opportunities and avoidance of potential market failures.

When assessing the costs of an MIS, the value of accurate, regular market information is difficult to estimate. Improved decision making of market managers can often save a company large amounts of money in the long-run. When assessing the value of MIS data, you should consider the costs of product development, marketing, and distribution.

MISs do not require highly sophisticated computer technology. There are many cost-effective ways to design a system for regular gathering, analysis, and dissemination of timely market information. At the simplest level, all that might be required is an effective assessment of information requirements, a filing cabinet, a well-designed method of data gathering and analysis, and a means of information distribution.

It is important to estimate a cost budget and time schedule for the creation of an MIS. The budget should effectively assess the comparative costs of proposed system designs and all potential costs. You should assess the:

- Time costs of system designers;

- Time costs of all management and company personnel involved in system development;

- Costs of obtaining required information; and

- Storage, processing, and data presentation costs.

These costs should then be loaded and weighed against perceived and known benefits derived by using the system. A time schedule for implementing the system should take into account competing demands on the time of the system design and support staff. If purchased information and secondary data are to be a feature of the MIS, the costs of acquiring the data must also be integrated into the estimate of system costs.

The worksheet outlined in Figure 9-3 allows you to estimate potential costs involved in establishing the MIS. Small-, medium-, and large-sized companies are addressed separately because of differences in information and budgetary requirements.

Figure 9-3
MIS Budget Considerations

Potential Budget Items	Small Company	Medium Company	Large Company
1. Staffing	$ _____	$ _____	$ _____
System designers	_____	_____	_____
Research staff	_____	_____	_____
Management personnel	_____	_____	_____
2. Equipment	$ _____	$ _____	$ _____
Personal computers	_____	_____	_____
Mainframes	_____	_____	_____
Filing systems	_____	_____	_____
3. Information Costs	$ _____	$ _____	$ _____
Primary data			
Surveys	_____	_____	_____
Secondary data			
Internal	_____	_____	_____
External	_____	_____	_____
4. Information	$ _____	$ _____	$ _____
Transmission	_____	_____	_____
5. Totals	$ _____	$ _____	$ _____

Proposed MIS Framework

The MIS you design will rely heavily on the size of your company. In other words, the size of the business will dictate the structure of the MIS.

Small-sized Companies

Small companies can benefit from an MIS. Acquisition, storage, processing, and dispersal of information can be tailored to meet the needs of the smaller company. If yours is a small company with limited resources and informational requirements, it is especially inadvisable to attempt a broad-based MIS from the start.

Planning should be done in stages using a block stacking approach, with each discrete block representing a specific information requirement. For a small company it will be necessary to segregate discrete blocks and assess which information requirements essential to your business are within budget constraints. After necessary information subsystems have been identified, an appropriate MIS can be designed via the steps previously outlined.

When your business experiences growth, the same building-block approach can be used to expand the MIS in line with your requirements and budget constraints. A disaggregated file system is advocated for even the smallest companies, to permit expansion of the MIS as the needs of the company change.

Market research facilities of most small companies are limited. Therefore, the framework illustrated in Figure 9-4 is comparatively uncomplicated.

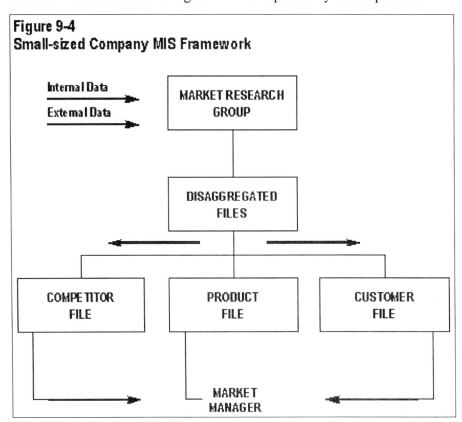

Figure 9-4
Small-sized Company MIS Framework

Internal and external data flows are gathered by the market research group or individual and segregated into categories such as competitor, product, and customer data. The data will address issues of importance in your decision making process.

Sorted data is posted to disaggregated data files and made available to the market manager to facilitate decision making. This simple system allows only limited information and performance feedback due to the assumed limitations of smaller company resources.

For a small company with no existing MIS, a limited budget and resource availability, the best place to start is to adequately determine your company's minimum information requirements. It is wise to divide information into internal and external data categories because in ideal circumstances the information is used differently.

Start with a filing cabinet(s) and set up a system of disaggregated files for areas of related interest, such as sales, end-users, and competitor profile information. As data is acquired, post it to the files manually and pass the data on to marketing decision makers. Keep up to date with the information needs and requirements of the marketing group. Set up a structure allowing their information needs to be passed on to you on a regular basis, such as regular meetings.

An adequate MIS can be rapidly organized if these simple steps are followed. The framework is extremely simple, flexible, and highly adaptable as the needs of the company change.

Medium-sized Companies

The requirements for an effective marketing information system differ by type of company. The institutional framework of small- and medium-sized companies differ as do their budget constraints. Medium-sized companies are usually able to budget and support a more complex system allowing more comprehensive information flows.

Organizing the information function to ensure effective vertical and horizontal information flows to and from the information unit is a primary concern.

Using the building-block approach described earlier, the market information system can be tailored to meet the needs of a medium- sized company. In the example illustrated in Figure 9-5, a market research group gathers and processes relevant internal and external data. The evaluated and abstracted data is stored in disaggregated data files. Data is distributed to marketing management in regular reports, reports specially requested by marketing decision makers, and irregular reports. Marketing decision makers then use the data to make a wide variety of decisions.

The system advocated for the mid-sized company is slightly more comprehensive and permits more elaborate return information flow between marketing decision makers and the market research group than does the small company system. These return flows may consist of requests for certain data and performance feedback, which would allow the market research group to assess the efficiency of information being forwarded to decision makers.

Large-sized Companies

The problems arising in a large-sized company attempting to establish an MIS framework are generally more challenging than those confronted by smaller companies. Larger budgets and resources are available to large companies, but their information requirements are generally more diverse due to broader product lines, larger marketing groups, and numerous divisions, departments, and subsidiaries.

If yours is a large-sized company, you should have no difficulty in organizing a marketing-department based MIS group and structuring the information function. The chief problem is instituting procedures and developing thorough systems to facilitate data flow throughout the marketing group. Training management in the use of the MIS has also been reported as a significant problem in large companies.

The ideal MIS framework for the large company involves input coming from all levels of management via systematized, established procedures.

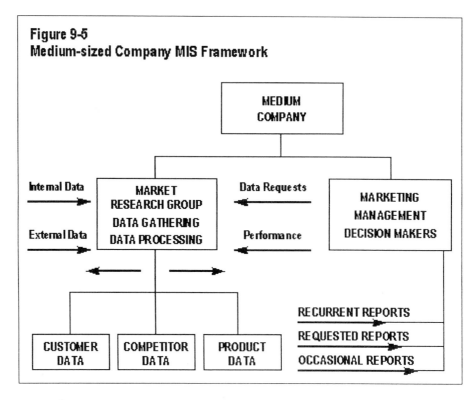

The information unit within the marketing group will check and analyze all available information to determine where in the company organization to transmit the data for storage and potential future use. This precludes data sent to groups within a company that have little use for it.

Using a Computer

In a small-sized company with limited product lines and information requirements, a computer is not a prerequisite of an effective marketing system. Often a basic system of disaggregated data files can be maintained manually without the use of computers. In medium- to large-sized companies, data requirements are far greater as is the diversity of information to be maintained. A computer is generally necessary for an effective MIS in a larger company environment.

A commonly encountered problem in larger companies is an MIS that has been poorly designed and developed piecemeal over significant periods of time. Each division of the company approaches the MIS in a different way so upper-management does not receive comparable reports from all divisions; thus, impacting efficient decision making.

Now that you have a good idea of what an MIS is and how you can implement one, you are ready to tackle output. The next section discusses the role of reports for your market research program.

Section 4

The Role of

R E P O R T S

Chapter 10

Presenting Report Results

Results of the research process can be presented either as an oral or a written report. Research reporting is probably the most vital stage of any research process. Despite a painstakingly thorough research process with exceedingly accurate results, poor reporting and communication of those results may lead to rejection by decision makers.

Reports are designed to assist decision makers. The role of the presentation — whether written or oral — is to effectively convey acquired information to the intended audience. If the report fails, the entire research process fails.

The quality of report content is determined during the research process. The written presentation of the report is often all that decision makers will see. Further, the report often is the sole means of evaluating the quality of the entire research effort. Throughout this chapter, you are given the key tips for an effective written presentation.

The primary goal of the written report is to effectively communicate the research project results to the intended report audience. A report should be clear, complete, and accurate. In addition, the individual(s) who write the report should have a clear sense of the intended audience.

If ideas or thoughts are unclear or vague, the report audience will have difficulty understanding and interpreting the report. Ensure that ideas are presented as clearly as possible by focusing on three areas — words, sentences and paragraphs.

The Role of Presentation

Four Written Presentation Tips

Tip #1 – Focus on Clarity

- Words — Remember that the words used in the report need to be concise, familiar, and unambiguous. Avoid using slang.

- Sentences — Structure sentences carefully. Pay close attention to wording, consistency of tense, and arrangement of ideas.

- Paragraphs — Ensure that each paragraph contains a single idea. Paragraphs should be suitably connected to allow a flow of ideas and should vary in length.

Tip #2 – Make it Complete

A report is considered complete when it provides the intended audience with required information in an understandable format.

Data contained in the report should address all issues and topics covered in the work assignment. Conclusions should be drawn based on report findings. A complete report will:

- Avoid excessive verbosity — Focus on concise definitions and short explanations; and

- Avoid excessive length — The desire to use all the information collected often encourages a large report. Use the intended audience's capabilities and primary areas of interest to determine the completeness of the report.

Tip #3 – Make Sure it Is Accurate

A thorough research process is the best way to ensure report accuracy. The finished report, no matter how well written, will not be accurate if the content is inaccurate.

The way a report is written can lead to inaccuracy and inconsistency. You can ensure written report accuracy by avoiding some common errors.

Inaccuracy in the report writing phase arises largely through:

- Poor handling or use of acquired data;

- Poor phrase structure;

- Illogical assumptions regarding knowledge of report users;

- Spelling mistakes;

- Poor punctuation;

- Illogical use of tenses; and

- Other grammar and syntax errors.

Be selective about what is included in the report and how it is used. Express thoughts clearly, using as few words and sentences as possible. Present important data in a pleasing visual format — use tables, charts, and graphs wherever appropriate to explain a concept or present figures.

The first draft of the report should be just that — a first draft. After drafting the report, thoroughly check for clarity, completeness, and accuracy.

A research report communicates ideas, conclusions, and findings to an audience. The market research report audience is generally made up of individuals directly responsible for the overall development of a company and its marketplace.

Tip #4 – Know Your Audience

The goal of the research project is to generate data to assist these decision makers by effectively conveying the results of the research project.

The primary reasons for preparing a research report are to:

- Expand knowledge of a company's market to improve its strategic position;

- Solve a specific strategic problem requiring new or greater knowledge about an industry or market;

- Obtain more knowledge about existing or potential competition;

- Obtain an objective, informed appraisal of where a market is headed;

- Acquire a firm in an unfamiliar industry; and

- Introduce a new or existing product into a new market.

When considering the audience requirements of the report, keep in mind the characteristics of your audience. Certain inherent characteristics of a market report audience are:

- The report audience — often management personnel — generally have little time to spare.

- The report audience is generally less concerned with the technical and logistical aspects of the research problem.

- The audience is generally unaware of the research methodology and the practical limitations of research.

- The characteristics and background of the report audience are as varied as individual audience members' reasons for examining the report.

You can design a top-notch report if you use the following essential tools.

Essential Report Format Tools

All research reports should be tightly organized, targeted toward the intended audience and the field of research. The following elements should be included to enhance efficiency, consistency, and clarity.

Tool #1 – A Title Page

A title page is necessary in all research reports. The content of the title page should show the following:

- Report title;

- Name of the group for whom the report was prepared;

- Date of report completion; and

- A list of individuals who should see the report.

A title page is essential even if the report is intended for limited distribution.

The report title page should indicate the nature of the research topic as clearly as possible.

Tool #2 – The Table of Contents

Even a brief report should contain a detailed table of contents. The table of contents should list, in order, the various segments and subsegments of the report.

A comprehensive list of all tables, figures, and charts should also be included on a separate page (or pages) immediately following the table of contents. The table of contents and list of figures at the front of this book provide an example of the content format.

Tool #3 – A Brief Summary

A brief summary provides an overview of the direction of a report, its areas of focus, and basic results. A summary should touch on the following factors contained in the body of the report:

- Report objectives,
- Major findings,
- Primary conclusions, and
- A brief synopsis of recommendations.

The summary is the most important part of the report. The summary should not attempt to abstract the entire report; it should be much more than a subject restatement or a brief synopsis of conclusions and recommendations. The summary should touch on all high points of the report and save your readers time while helping them understand.

Results outlined in the summary must be consistent with those contained in the body of the report. Only primary findings should be included in the summary. A good approach is to include two-line statements about each main finding contained in the body of the report.

Tool #4 – Introductory Comments

A report introduction provides your readers with the background information they need to understand the report.

The style, size, and structure of the introduction are dependent on the intended audience and the extent of their familiarity with the research topic. If the report is intended for a broad audience, a more extensive introduction is required. A report introduction should:

- Define common technical terms used in the report;
- Delineate market segments and subsegments;
- Define which manufacturers and products are considered competitors;
- Discuss history and explain why certain issues were addressed and how the structure of the report was determined; and
- State and discuss objectives of the research report. Any issues not included in the report should be described and reasons provided for their omission.

After reading the report introduction, your audience should have a complete knowledge of the research project objectives and have a strong feeling of the importance of the report and the primary research issues. The introduction should heighten the confidence of the reader in the report, its findings, and the research that went into putting it together.

Tool #5 – Body of the Report

The body of the report contains all the details and results of the research process. Details that should be included in the report are:

- Report methodology,
- Research limitations, and
- Research results.

Report methodology is difficult to communicate to the reader. Methodology information consists of:

- Research design,
- Methods used in data collection, and
- Sample information.

When describing the above information, do not overwhelm the audience with details. Avoid using highly technical jargon that may cause confusion.

Inform your readers of the research structure. For example, state whether you used exploratory or casual research techniques. Also, the report should state why a particular data collection method was chosen over available alternatives.

Explicit details about sample procedures are not required. The audience report should provide a minimum of information regarding the sample. Further information can always be provided if it is requested. Typically, you will want to provide:

- How the sample was selected;
- How the sample was surveyed; and
- Why one sample group was selected over another.

Research limitations should be discussed in the body of the report to enhance report credibility. A discussion of research limitations should include a brief analysis of the potential for limitations to impact results. If research limitations go unstated and are then discovered by the audience, the credibility of the report can be severely damaged.

Research findings should be as detailed and exacting as possible. The majority of the report should be result presentation and supporting figures and tables. When presenting research project results, be sure to:

- Address all research issues;

- Exclude all irrelevant information;

- Use graphs, charts, tables, and figures only when they can effectively help convey an idea;

- Describe any graphic material in the body of the report; and

- Use tables in the body of the report to summarize relevant information.

Tool #6 – Recommendations and Conclusions

In most instances conclusions should be provided from research findings. It is important to keep in mind the original report objectives to draw pertinent conclusions.

The conclusions and recommendations section of the report should be logically organized. Structure the section carefully so report objectives and conclusions are presented sequentially.

Make recommendations only when appropriate. Recommendations:

- Make the researcher commit to certain findings, enabling the report audience to get the most from the report;

- Force the researcher to continually consider the needs of the report audience; and

- May address specific report audience questions.

Tool #7 – Appendices

The appendix of the report is used to present information not presented in the body of the report. You should place information in an appendix instead of in the body of the report if:

- The data is too complicated to use in the body of the report;

- The information is excessively detailed; or

- The information is superfluous or unnecessary for the body of the report.

Detailed statistics, summaries of tables, sample design considerations, and other complex statistical information should be placed in the appendix. Generally, only technically experienced or highly interested readers will scan the appendix.

Tool #8 – Present Results Graphically

Graphs and charts should be used only when appropriate. Further, design considerations are of extreme importance.

When graphs are used excessively, inappropriately, or are poorly designed, they may actually confuse or disappoint the report audience. Charts are much more than a representation of values or quantities in graphic form. The charts preferred for market research reports are:

- Pie charts,

- Bar charts,

- Line charts, and

- Stratum charts.

Whatever chart you use, the picture must convey an understanding of the presented information.

Graphs are not the only way to present quantitative information. Tables and explanatory text can also be extremely effective.

Consider all options — certain readers do not like information presented graphically, judging it too technical and confusing.

If you follow the key tips for written presentation and use the eight essential tools, you will build a report of which you can be proud.

A Top-Quality Report

Notes

Chapter 11

Custom Market Research

Custom market research addresses a specific topic, completed by a specially contracted external research group or individual. Nearly all internal market research operations rely on external or purchased market research to some extent. Purchased market research services may include multiclient or custom (single-client) studies.

When multiclient or off-the-shelf research reports are available, current, and can meet the majority of the research project's requirements, you can use them over custom work to keep costs in line. However, often the market information required is far too specialized, specific, and detailed for a multiclient or off-the-shelf report. The market research budget should include some contingency for purchasing custom market research.

Budget allocation is highly dependent on the structure of your business. If your business is in a rapid expansion stage, a significant portion of the total market research budget should be allocated for custom market research needs.

Custom studies are often extremely effective in meeting specific information requirements. Custom studies should be used in certain situations, such as when:

- Vital information on the market, or a current multiclient or off-the-shelf study addressing the relevant issues, is not available.

- Multiclient and off-the-shelf reports lack sufficient detail to meet information requirements.

- The research topic is broad, requiring a mixture of internal and consultant staffs for adequate completion.
- No internal resources for addressing the topic exist.
- The project requires knowledge unavailable in-house.
- Using external researchers minimizes the potential for bias to impact project results.
- Project interest areas may be totally new to the company.
- Custom research projects can be completed rapidly to meet tight internal deadlines.

Defining the Project

The success of any custom market research project depends on the detail put in before the project begins. The primary factors to consider when determining the extent and specifications of the project are outlined in nine easy-to-follow steps.

- Step 1 — Define the research problem.
- Step 2 — Determine the information needed to solve the problem.
- Step 3 — Determine what research methods will be used.
- Step 4 — Budgeting considerations. Determine how the project will be funded and how large the funding will be.
- Step 5 — Time constraints. Determine total project length.
- Step 6 — Project management. Determine how consultants will be chosen and by whom.
- Step 7 — Decide who will be responsible for maintaining continued communication between consultants and the company and who will ensure that project goals are met.
- Step 8 — Report format. Decide how research results will be presented at the completion of the study. Decide how to structure the report to best meet company needs.
- Step 9 — Staffing. Decide the structure of the consulting group. Determine what tasks must be performed for project completion and who will be responsible for completing each task.

If project parameters are insufficiently defined at inception, opportunities for inadequate communication with consultants and confusion during the research process will increase. Devote time to carefully designing the entire custom consulting process, and organize details of the project.

The Search Is on

A written custom project outline is invaluable during a search for consultants to complete the project. It also helps minimize opportunities for ambiguities to arise during the project.

Ensure that all elements to cover in the project are clearly specified. Also, indicate the detail of research you desire — an inadequately detailed report will be useless. Specify graphs and tables to include in the project. Detail the desired content of forecasts, the desired length of the forecast period, and the need for sales forecast in both unit shipments and dollar revenues. Highly-detailed custom studies can be several times more costly than a custom study with limited detail.

The minimum factors to address in a custom study include:

- Base year market numbers for relevant products;
- Forecasts for a specified time period;
- Technology forecasts in relevant fields — or expected predominant product characteristics and demands for product development;
- Detailed competitive analysis and market share;
- End-user analysis; and
- Detailed segmentation of potential markets into markets and submarkets.

A considerable portion of custom studies address extremely specific and specialized topics; so a single project format will not be suitable for all occasions.

In addition to specifying the required project detail, be sure to indicate any product areas or market segments to cover less extensively. Some products may not actively compete with your own products now, but may do so in the future.

There are several areas of information to include in the study in addition to the extent of detail required.

- End users — Areas of product end-use and potential applications should be clearly defined and listed.
- Technology — All technologies should be listed for analysis and forecasting. Any special requirements, such as analysis of research and development funding of various firms, should also be used for analysis.
- Extent of forecasts — The detail of forecasts required should be specified. (Should dollar forecasts account for inflation or should they be in constant dollars?)
- To what extent will competitors be analyzed? How many competitors will be covered? Are forecasts of projected competitor market shares and estimates of their activities in particular market segments needed?

Consultant Selection — Be Wise!

After you have decided to use custom market research, and the extent and detail of the project has been outlined in writing, you are now ready to identify the consultant for the project.

Comparative costs between sources differ extensively and each source offers its own advantages and disadvantages. The decision on which source to use should be based on specific information requirements. The types of custom research vendors available are:

- Market research organizations;
- Advertising agencies and accounting firms;
- Independent consultants; and
- Management consultants.

Market Research Organizations

Market research organizations offer a distinct advantage because they focus exclusively on market research. Market research companies have developed significant methodology skills, considerable knowledge, and expertise in the areas in which they specialize. Some market research groups focus on single areas of specialty, such as consumer products or industrial goods, while others focus on several areas or fields.

The significant in-house databases offered by market research companies allow them to generally conduct research in greater depth and detail than available alternative sources. The staff and resources offered by market research companies are generally stable and available, particularly when they are compared to smaller independent consulting operations. Training time is not usually required if an experienced market research team is used.

Fees charged by market research companies for consulting services are about half those charged by management consultants. The comprehensive services and reliability these organizations offer are equal, if not superior, to those of management consultants.

Market research organizations can also be differentiated in terms of the geographical scope of their coverage. Organizations may focus on regional, national, or international markets. The scopes of coverage available are outlined in Figure 11-1.

Advertising Agencies and Accounting Firms

Advertising agencies frequently conduct market research for their clients. The extent of market research conducted by advertising agencies usually consists of either mail, telephone, or personal interviews.

This type of research is commonly limited to fairly unsophisticated issues such as brand name preference. The primary disadvantages of using advertising agencies as sources of market research are:

- The technical experience and expertise of advertising agency researchers is often limited;
- Questionnaire design, data processing background, and skills may be lacking; and
- Advertising agencies are often biased, reflecting efforts to see advertising budgets increased.

Fees charged by advertising agencies for these services are typically low. The market research is generally conducted as a service to the client, with the principal source of revenue being derived from the advertising contract.

Figure 11-1
Differing Geographical Scope of Market Research Firms

Regional organizations. Market research firms that focus only on regional markets are extremely rare (particularly nonexistent). In the early stages of the development of their consulting services, independent consultants occasionally tend to focus solely on regional markets.

National organizations. National market research companies generally focus on markets in their own country, although analysts may be sent to other countries on special projects.

National firms. National firms exhibit significant specialization in certain fields. These firms, typically smaller in size than international companies, offer specialization and expertise in certain areas as their principal advantage.

International organizations. International market research organizations have offices in at least two major geographical markets they address — such as the U.S. and Europe. These companies include SRI International, Frost and Sullivan, Macintosh, and Arthur D. Little.

Accounting firms typically suffer considerable drawbacks in terms of their capability to conduct custom market research, generally focusing on financial issues and considerations. Their experience in primary data gathering and their research methodology are often limited. Also, the cost of this custom research can be great.

Independent Consultants

Independent consultants vary widely in experience, capability, availability, and degree of competence. Independent consultants can be classified into three broad categories.

- Full-time professional consultants with several years experience;

- Individuals doing consulting work between jobs until full-time employment becomes available. These consultants often have no long-term commitment to market research consulting; and

- Part-time consultants with a long-term commitment to market research and consulting, but who do so in their spare time (may be retired or moonlighting).

Full-time consultants can generally apply themselves exclusively to the demands of your research project. Certain drawbacks typically limit the quality of the custom research produced by independent consultants. Independents can be unreliable, have limited equipment at their disposal, and may use poor research methodology.

Generally, independents focus on particular fields of interest where they have developed a significant specialty. If a research topic is extremely broad-based, an independent consultant may have difficulty completing the project within a given timeframe.

Finding a between-jobs consultant with expertise in the field you wish to examine is not impossible. Gauging the competence of the consultant may be more difficult. If the consultant has had comparatively little experience, determining his or her ability to complete the project is complicated.

Despite any significant experience, the between-jobs consultant may have in the relevant field, he or she remains an unknown quantity in terms of consulting capability.

Between-jobs independent consultants are generally readily available to begin a project immediately, but the consultant's capacity to provide follow-up information over significant periods may be limited.

Part-time consultants can generally be contracted to conduct custom research for a comparatively low fee. Locating them can be difficult — if consultants are moonlighting, their available time may be limited and can fluctuate as their full-time job demands vary.

A specialized, independent, part-time consultant can often be relied on for completing a highly specific project without a tight timeframe. If a custom project requires a tight deadline, do not use a part-time independent consultant.

Management Consultants

Management consulting groups vary widely in terms of size, specialty, and capacity. The extent of management consulting specialization differs widely among groups. Some groups focus on specific industries and markets, while others focus on a broad range of high-tech arenas and employ staff with highly developed expertise in each area.

Management consultants operate differently from market research organizations and may lack experience with market research methods. These groups generally analyze the complete joint operations of their clients, examining external influences and potential markets, and recommend appropriate strategies for success. Research fees are generally very high.

Decisions, Decisions

Market research is an extremely difficult exercise. Accurate data collection is the cornerstone of the entire research process. A high proportion of research projects are inadequately executed by inexperienced internal staff or poorly qualified part-time consultants.

When you need an accurate and complete research project, select a company specializing in the market research process. This can make a difference in the quality of the completed project.

The role of management consultants tends to be at the chief executive officer (CEO) level. That is, CEOs are experts in focusing on the overall strategic direction of the company and the issues and problems impacting management. These consultants typically assume that the information required for their analysis is already available.

Data collection is not an area of management consultant specialty. On longer, more broadly-based projects, management consultants often use market research organizations to accumulate the data required to complete their analysis.

Figure 11-2 highlights the strengths and weaknesses of custom consulting services.

Figure 11-2
Strengths and Weaknesses of Custom Consulting Sources

Market Research Organizations

- Excellent methodology techniques;
- High levels of technical expertise;
- Excellent staff quality and reliability;
- Generally readily available for project completion; and
- Fees are usually mid-range.

Advertising Agencies and Accounting Firms

- Methodology techniques are not typically well-developed;
- Technical expertise tends to be fairly low;
- Satisfactory staff quality and reliability;
- Generally readily available for project completion; and
- Fees are usually lower as the research is part of a strategy to attract advertising revenues.

Independent Consultants

- Good to excellent methodology techniques;
- Fair levels of technical expertise;
- Fair staff quality, occasionally unreliable;
- Fair availability for project completion;
- Generally lack resources; and
- Fees are typically low- to mid-range.

Management Consultants

- Fair levels of technical expertise;
- Excellent staff quality and reliability;
- Excellent availability for project completion; and
- Fees are usually extremely high.

Proposal Evaluation — Four Key Steps

You may seem overwhelmed by a stack of proposals that tell you what certain companies can do for you. You can easily evaluate these proposals by following four simple steps.

Step 1 — Check References

When selecting a source for a custom consulting project, use extreme care and forethought. Employ every means available to check on the ability of the custom research group to meet project requirements. The primary methods to check references of a potential custom project consulting group include:

- Previous reports. Review several previous reports completed by the potential custom consultant group. Pay close attention to report format, presentation, and levels of detail

- Repeat business. Try to determine the extent of repeat business the potential custom consulting group has acquired in recent periods. This serves as a good indication of the success it has had in satisfying clients.

- Credit check. Run a credit check on any potential custom consulting source to determine its stability.

- Previous client check. Previous clients can assist in providing a fairly good picture of the potential custom consulting group's performance.

- History of the company. Focus on how many years it has been in business, the total company size, and company growth.

Step 2 — Inspect the Facility

A tour of the facilities of the potential custom research consulting group can provide some indication of the likelihood of its ability to meet project needs. During a facility inspection, ask yourself:

- In what type of office is the proposed custom consulting group working? Is it operating out of a home or a permanent office facility?

- How large is the staff at the facility? Ask how many of the staff are permanent, full-time employees and how many are part-time workers?

- Does the facility contain a comprehensive in-house database of information? Does it have a comprehensive in-house library?

The answers to these questions may give you an idea of the group's capabilities to meet your needs.

Step 3 — Review Proposed Research Team Members

The capabilities and qualities of the research staff are the primary factor determining the overall quality of the report. When reviewing members of the proposed research team, focus on their individual strengths and levels of reliability and stability.

Read the resumes of each proposed member of the research team and take careful notes on each. Compare these notes to those of alternative research groups. When assessing the overall quality of proposed team members, ask yourself:

- How long has each proposed member of the research team been associated with the proposed custom consulting group?

- Have they demonstrated a significant degree of reliability with this and other employers?
- Do any or all of the proposed team members specialize or have relevant expertise in the research topic?

Be critical when examining the background of each proposed team member. If one of them drops out before project completion, the information compiled by that member may be lost.

When various consulting groups submit proposals, make sure they submit the names of the project director, all analysts, and support people to be involved in the project. If the structure of the support team outlined in the proposal is acceptable, insist on a clause in the contract that states any changes in the team structure must first be approved by you.

The methodology the potential consulting group intends to use should be clearly explained in the project proposal. Issues on which to focus to determine the intended report methodology are outlined in the worksheet in Figure 11-3.

Step 4 — Understand the Proposed Methodology

Figure 11-3
Worksheet to Determine a Research Group's Methodology

Which secondary data sources does the custom research group intend to use?

_____

How will the secondary data sources be used? _____

What percentage of total research will be accounted for by primary research? ____

_____

What will comprise primary research? _____

What percentage will be made up of personal, telephone, and mail interviews? ____

_____

Who will be the sources of primary data? _____

☐   Company executives

☐   Marketing personnel

☐   Industry experts

☐   Product engineers

You can play a significant role in the custom market research project. It is essential that you or an assigned individual from your staff manage the project. You can successfully accomplish this by following the helpful hints on the next two pages.

Successfully Manage the Project

Clearly Understand the Project Scope

Develop a clear understanding with the custom consulting group so the final report provides the required information. The only way to effectively create this understanding is to write a detailed and specific plan as discussed previously. Send the potential consulting group this work statement before receiving its research proposal.

Negotiations with the consulting group should only begin after your work statement has been reviewed. The work specification should detail the scheduling, nature, and extent of meetings to be held with the consulting group while the report is in progress. The consultants should have a clear series of goals to attain by each scheduled meeting so project progress can be assessed.

If unfamiliar with the potential consulting group company, schedule a meeting after receiving its proposal, but before signing the research contract. The meeting should determine whether the consultant has an adequate understanding of the scope of the project and has developed a satisfactory methodology for completion. Go over the research specifications point by point to ensure no ambiguities exist regarding project structure. Go through the proposed report methodology with the consulting personnel to assure its adequacy.

Ensure Followup with Meetings and Progress Report Format

Frequent meetings and progress reports with the custom consulting group help determine if research is progressing on schedule and according to the work plan.

These regular meetings assist in discovering any problems that may have arisen, allowing you to help solve them before the report is completed and the damage is irreversible.

The number of meetings held will depend on the total length of the project. If it is scheduled to last three months, three meetings should be scheduled — one per month until project completion. Regular telephone calls can also monitor the progress of the project. Before submission of the final report, a meeting should be held to proof the report and look for any areas not adequately addressed or aspects of the report presentation that are unsatisfactory.

Instruct Your Staff to Cooperate with the Research Group

The research project will run more efficiently if you offer the full cooperation of your organization. If the custom consultants require regular meetings with members of your staff, these should be readily provided. In-house data may assist in project completion and should also be made available.

Occasionally, a business will permit members of its own market research staff to assist the custom consulting group in completing its project. This may help your company gain a better understanding of the results of the completed project. Your own market research staff may also benefit from any pointers, ideas, or training they may receive from the consultants.

Often companies have strong reservations about providing cooperation and information to the custom consulting group. The primary fear is that the researcher will merely reproduce the information in the final report. If caution has been exercised in selecting the custom consulting group, there should be no ethical concerns.

The report presentation is a key indication of whether the report has been valuable in answering research questions and if your project budget money has been well spent. It is common practice for the presentation to occur two to five weeks after completion of the project and receipt of the final report.

The consulting group should provide enough copies of the report so all concerned staff members can review it and note any questions they might have. Key personnel in your business impacted by the report findings should thoroughly review the report before the scheduled presentation. When examining and reviewing the completed report, look for whether:

- All the issues specified in the work statement have been adequately addressed;

- The conclusions and recommendations reached in the report are supported in the body of the report;

- The research methodology and process are adequately explained and outlined;

- Charts and tables are accurate and clear, with text supporting the graphics; and

- Any glaring errors or inconsistencies exist in the text or the charts.

All company personnel responsible for reviewing the report should list questions or comments — both positive and negative — that they have about the report. Comments and questions should be formatted into a single document, excluding irrelevant or redundant comments or questions, and forwarded to the individual(s) communicating with the custom consultants. The list should be given to the custom consulting group for review before the presentation session. The presentation should be organized in the following manner:

- The speaking consultant should begin the presentation by reviewing the principal conclusions of the research project. This familiarizes everyone present with the report content.

- The consultant should reply to each question in the question and comment list sent to him or her.

- There should be an open forum to allow the report audience to voice any additional questions.

- Carefully note issues the consultant fails to adequately address for later consideration and discussion.

After the final presentation session, maintain contact with the custom consulting group to make sure any remaining ambiguities and issues are addressed.

Know What to Expect from the Final Report Presentation

Notes

Chapter 12

Off-the-Shelf Market Research

Off-the-shelf reports are a form of external or purchased market research. Typically, off-the-shelf or syndicated research services consist of broadly-based market research studies. The reports are broad so they can effectively meet the market information needs of a wide range of potential clients.

Off-the-shelf reports differ from multiclient market research although the two terms are often used interchangeably. Off-the-shelf reports generally focus on a particular industry or marketplace but have no specific intended audience — their potential audience consists of anyone with an interest in the research topic. Multiclient reports are generally prepared according to requirements designated by 10 to 15 specific clients.

Off-the-shelf market research must be organized to fit management methodology. If your company has an internal market research group, off-the-shelf reports can provide ongoing data for analysis.

Advantages of Off-the-Shelf Market Research

Company market research staffs designed and structured to conduct continuous monitoring, forecasting, and planning in particular product areas and markets can make extensive use of well-organized off-the-shelf research. For these organizations, off-the-shelf reports should be used to supplement the internal research function.

Off-the-shelf reports can provide important industry background, technology, and market trend information. Data in these reports can be compared to internal research staff findings.

An internal market research staff designed for quick reaction in highly volatile markets can also make extensive use of off-the-shelf research. Subscriptions to syndicated report services can help this type of market research staff maintain a comprehensive, ongoing database of market information designed to enable the internal market research staff to complete detailed studies rapidly and effectively.

When budgeting annual market research funds, always consider the extent of existing market research and how it can meet your research needs. Off-the-shelf reports are often the least expensive research alternative and should always be actively considered.

Also, consider how to augment your own internal market research with off-the-shelf reports. Extensive use of relevant off-the-shelf reports can effectively reduce the need for and cost of internal market research and custom consulting services.

Figure 12-1 outlines the primary advantages and disadvantages of off-the-shelf research.

When to Use Off-the-shelf Market Research

Off-the-shelf market research report purchases have increased over the past 20 years. The quality of off-the-shelf market research varies widely among suppliers.

The ideal market research program combines internal and purchased external services. The primary difficulty with this approach is determining the ideal mixture of off-the-shelf, custom, and internal research. Methods used will vary depending on the type of company and company growth trends and objectives.

Any market research requiring comprehensive industry and market background or product or growth trend research, or both, should use applicable off-the-shelf market research.

The decision to use off-the-shelf market research depends on several distinct factors. Ask yourself:

- What are the time constraints on the research project?

- Are internal market staff members available to complete the project?

- Can the off-the-shelf report supplier provide the necessary information within the time constraints?

- Does the off-the-shelf report fit your budget?

The choice of off-the-shelf market research is much easier if details regarding the content and costs of the research are available. Off-the-shelf research suppliers generally provide detailed outlines of their research reports and a listing of the report costs, usually in the form of a catalog.

How to Evaluate Research Quality

The most important factor when purchasing off-the-shelf market research is that the reports be broad enough to meet the general needs of a wide variety of clients.

Figure 12-1
Summary of the Advantages and Disadvantages of
Off-the-shelf Market Research

Advantages

- Reports are often immediately available.

- Research is flexible and can be used when needed to control market research costs.

- Research is generally inexpensive compared to available research alternatives.

- Research provides access to a wide variety of information.

- Methodology of Off-the-shelf reports is generally extremely reliable.

- Reports allow the user to accumulate comprehensive databases.

Disadvantages

- You have little control over the research methodology.

- You have little control over the scope of the research report.

- Some effort is required to locate and evaluate suppliers of market research.

Do not expect an off-the-shelf study to meet all the detail requirements of your research questions. If explicit detail in the research project is required, either perform the research in-house and support it with off-the-shelf research, or commission a custom study.

Off-the-shelf market information is advantageous because it can provide valuable material at a competitive cost. These reports can provide information on:

- Product, technology, general industry, and market trends;

- Historic market figures and forecasts;

- Market share information; and

- Information on mergers, acquisitions, or takeovers that may affect the industry.

Off-the-shelf market research can be purchased before or after you write an in-house report. Catalogs circulated by report suppliers provide an indication of the stage of research.

If an off-the-shelf report has not yet been started, you may be able to influence the research scope to include issues you feel may be valid. Prepare a list of your more general information requirements and negotiate for their inclusion in the off-the-shelf report. Most market research firms are more than willing to consider subscriber input when assembling research reports.

If an off-the-shelf report has already been completed, examine the table of contents very carefully before purchasing it to ensure that the majority of your general interest areas are addressed.

After acquiring an off-the-shelf report, choose a familiar subject area and examine that section of the report. If you find discrepancies, request that they be explained in some detail. When assessing the quality of an off-the-shelf report, look for the following key elements.

- Data in the report should be consistent with your knowledge of the subject matter. Note any discrepancies and request elaboration.

- The writing style should be clear and concise. Check for spelling and grammatical errors, and examine all technical terms to ensure consistency.

- There should be no significant errors in charts or tables. Charts and tables should be referred to in the text.

- Text and graphics should be clear. Examine the quality of print and graphics.

Look for Quality

There is often a tradeoff among vendors of off-the-shelf reports between quality and speed. If the report was hastily prepared it will be reflected in a lack of quality. A quality off-the-shelf research report does not have to be perfect, but it should be consistent throughout.

Language used in the report is a vital consideration — if the writer uses an overblown writing style it may indicate a lack of understanding of the research topic. The writer should demonstrate a good working knowledge of the industry's accepted technical terminology. If the table of contents does not use correct technical terminology or fails to focus on relevant issues, it generally points to a report of bad quality.

To further assure a high-quality report, check whether the writer has named all major competitors in each market segment. This is a primary issue of concern; it is essential to know who the major market players are and have an idea of their market share.

A good indicator of the level of report detail is the number of companies in the market actually mentioned in the report. Check to see that all company names are spelled correctly. Develop a list of all competitors mentioned in the report, checking it against your knowledge to verify its accuracy.

Index

Preview! New business books and tools from The Oasis Press.

Finally, a one-stop answer book for your questions about business corporations. Saves time with your attorney. Saves hours in the library. Tells what you need to know to avoid personal liability and legal pitfalls. A "must" whether you already own a small business corporation, or plan to form one.
Paperback $19.95

From the editors at The Oasis Press comes this guide for the beginning business owner. This all-in-one book lists the major requirements and issues a new business owner needs to know, including
• Start-up financing
• Creating a business plan
• Marketing strategies
• Environmental laws
Checklists and Plans of Action ensure that you have "all the bases" covered.

New updated edition!
Our best seller for 13 years — still your best source of practical business information. Find out what new laws affect your business. Now there's an edition for every state in the U.S., plus the District of Columbia.
Paperback $24.95
Binder Workbook Edition $29.95
Specify which state(s) you want on your order.

The old adage says that the only certainties in life are death and taxes. While one may be beyond your control, you can use recent tax law changes to your certain financial advantage. This new book covers every tax break now available in today's "reformed" tax environment.
Paperback $14.95

197 forms to get your people hired, your sales recorded, your product shipped, your cash flowing, your customers accounted for and your organization organized. Get the forms that pilot goods, people, services, and numbers through the business day.
Paperback $19.95
Expanded Binder Edition $49.95

Your people expect leadership. Let them know where you stand and where they stand using clear policies. This newly expanded book gives you 65 written model policies plus alternates. Covers sexual harassment, AIDS, privacy, and other sensitive issues. Includes 20 forms.
Paperback $29.95
Binder Edition $49.95
Software for IBM & MAC available, too.

Get business tips from over 157 seasoned experts.

Business Formation and Planning

**Start Your Business:
A Beginner's Guide**

 Book

This handy, easy-to-read book is full of checklists to help answer your start-up questions. Helps you ask the right questions and find out where you can get the answers. The Plan of Action Worksheets make it easy to compile and coordinate your to-do list. The book is divided into sections covering business, legal, marketing, human resources, sales, taxes, and other decisions.

**The Successful Business
Plan: Secrets & Strategies**

 Book and software
for IBM & compatibles

Start-to-finish guide on creating a successful business plan. Includes tips from venture capitalists, bankers, and successful CEOs. Features worksheets for ease in planning and budgeting with the Abrams Method of Flow-Through Financials. Gives a sample business plan, plus specialized help for retailers, service companies, manufacturers, and in-house corporate plans. Also tells how to find funding sources.

**Starting and Operating a
Business in... series**
Book available for each state in the
United States, plus District of Columbia

One-stop resource to current federal and state laws and regulations that affect businesses. Clear "human language" explanations of complex issues, plus samples of government forms, and sources for additional help or information. Helps seasoned business owners keep up with changing legislation, and guides new entrepreneurs step-by-step to start and run the business. Includes many checklists and worksheets to organize ideas, create action plans, and project financial scenarios.

**The Essential Corporation
Handbook**

 Book

This comprehensive reference for small business corporations in all 50 states and Washington, D.C. explains the legal requirements for maintaining a corporation in good standing. Features many sample corporate documents which are annotated by the author to show what to look for and what to look out for. Tells how to avoid personal liability as an officer, director, or shareholder.

**Surviving and Prospering
in a Business Partnership**

 Book

From evaluation of potential partners, through the drafting of agreements, to day-to-day management of working relationships, this book helps avoid classic partnership catastrophes. Discusses how to set up the partnership to reduce the financial and emotional consequences of unanticipated disputes, dishonesty, divorce, disability, or death of a partner.

**California Corporation
Formation Package and
Minute Book**

 Book and software
for IBM & Mac

Provides forms required for incorporating and maintaining closely held corporations, including: articles of incorporation; bylaws; stock certificates, stock transfer record sheets, bill of sale agreement; minutes form; plus many others. Addresses questions on fees, timing, notices, regulations, election of directors and other critical factors. Software has minutes, bylaws, and articles of incorporation already for you to edit and customize (using your own word processor).

**Franchise Bible:
A Comprehensive Guide**

 Book (New edition)

Complete guide to franchising for prospective franchisees or for business owners considering franchising their business. Includes actual sample documents, such as a complete offering circular, plus worksheets for evaluating franchise companies, locations, and organizing information before seeing an attorney. This book is helpful for lawyers as well as their clients.

Home Business Made Easy

 Book

Thinking of starting a business at home? This book is the easiest road to starting a home business. Shows you how to select and start a home business that fits your interests, lifestyle and pocketbook. Walks you through 153 different businesses you could operate from home full or part time. Author David Hanania has boiled the process down to simple steps so you can get started now to realize your dreams.

The Small Business Expert
Software for IBM-PC & compatibles

Generates comprehensive custom checklist of the state and federal laws and regulations based on your type and size of business. Allows comparison of doing business in each of the 50 states. Built-in worksheets create outlines for personnel policies, marketing feasibility studies, and a business plan draft. *Requires 256K RAM and hard disk.*

**Starting and Operating a
Business: U.S. Edition**
Set of eleven binders

The complete encyclopedia of how to do business in the U.S. Describes laws and regulations for each state, plus Washington, D.C., as well as the federal government. Includes lists of sources of help, plus post cards for requesting materials from government agencies. This set is valuable for businesses with locations or marketing activities in several states, plus franchisors, attorneys, and other consultants.

To order these business tools, use the enclosed order form, FAX 503-476-1479 or call us toll-free at 800-228-2275

Step-by-step techniques for generating more profit.

Financial Management

Top Tax Saving Ideas for Today's Small Business

Second edition available Spring 1995

An extensive summary of every imaginable tax break that is still available in today's "reformed" tax environment. Deals with the various entities that the owner/manager may choose to operate a business. Identifies a wide assortment of tax deduction, fringe benefits, and tax deferrals. Includes a simplified checklist of recent tax law changes with an emphasis on tax breaks.

Financial Management Techniques for Small Business

Book and software for IBM-PC & compatibles

Clearly reveals the essential ingredients of sound financial management in detail. By monitoring trends in your financial activities, you will be able to uncover potential problems before they become crises. You'll understand why you can be making a profit and still not have the cash to meet expenses, and you'll learn the steps to change your business' cash behavior to get more return for your effort. Software makes your business' financial picture graphically clear, and lets you look at "what if" scenarios.

The Buyer's Guide to Business Insurance

New Book

Straightforward advice on shopping for insurance, understanding types of coverage, comparing proposals and premium rates. Worksheets help identify and weigh the risks a particular business is likely to face, then determine if any of those might be safely self-insured or eliminated. Request for proposal form helps businesses avoid over-paying for protection.

Collection Techniques for a Small Business

New Book

Practical tips on how to turn receivables into cash. Worksheets and checklists help businesses establish credit policies, track accounts, and flag when it is necessary to bring in a collection agency, attorney, or go to court. This book advises how to deal with disputes, negotiate settlements, win in small claims court, and collect on judgments. Gives examples of telephone collection techniques and collection letters.

Secrets to Buying & Selling a Business

New Book
(Available Spring 1994)

Prepares a business buyer or seller for negotiations that will achieve win-win results. Shows how to determine the real worth of a business, including intangible assets such as "goodwill." Over 36 checklists and worksheets on topics such as tax impact on buyers and sellers, escrow checklist, cash flow projections, evaluating potential buyers, financing options, and many others.

Business Owner's Guide to Accounting & Bookkeeping

Book

Makes understanding the economics of business simple. Explains the basic accounting principles that relate to any business. Step-by-step instructions for generating accounting statements and interpreting them, spotting errors, and recognizing warning signs. Discusses how banks and other creditors view financial statements.

Controlling Your Company's Freight Costs
Book

Shows how to increase company profits by trimming freight costs. Provides tips for comparing alternative methods and shippers, then negotiating contracts to receive the most favorable discounts. Tells how to package shipments for safe transport. Discusses freight insurance and dealing with claims for loss or damage. Appendices include directory of U.S. ports, shipper's guide, and sample bill of lading.

Financial Templates

Software for IBM-PC & compatibles

Calculates and graphs many business "what-if" scenarios and financial reports. Twenty-eight financial templates such as income statements, cash flow, and balance sheet comparisons, break-even analyses, product contribution comparisons, market share, net present value, sales model, pro formas, loan payment projections, etc. *Requires 512K RAM hard disk or two floppy drives, plus Lotus 1-2-3 or compatible spreadsheet program.*

Yes, we accept credit cards — VISA, MasterCard, American Express, Discover, or your personal or business check.

Proven tools and ideas to expand your business.

Marketing & Public Relations

Power Marketing

Book

A wealth of basic, how-to marketing information that easily takes a new or experienced business owner through the essentials of marketing and sales strategies, customer database marketing, advertising, public relations, budgeting, and follow-up marketing systems. Written in a friendly tone by a marketing educator, the book features worksheets with step-by-step instructions, a glossary of marketing terms, and a sample marketing plan. Also available: *Power Marketing Tools for Small Business*—two hours of audio tapes by author Jody Hornor that reveal 81 tools you can use to increase your market power.

How To Develop & Market Creative Business Ideas

Book

Step-by-step manual guides the inventor through all stages of new product development. Discusses patenting your invention, trademarks, copyrights, and how to construct your prototype. Gives information on financing, distribution, test marketing, and finding licensees. Plus, lists many useful sources for prototype resources, trade shows, funding, and more.

Know Your Market: How to do Low-Cost Market Research

Book

Workbook explains how a small business can conduct its own market research. Shows how to set objectives, determine which techniques to use, create a schedule, and then monitor expenses. Encompasses primary research (trade shows, telephone interviews, mail surveys), plus secondary research (using available information in print).

Customer Information and Tracking System (CITS)
Software for IBM-PC & compatibles

💾

Stores details of past activities plus future reminders on customers, clients, contacts, vendors, and employees, then gives instant access to that information when needed. "Tickler" fields keep reminders of dates for recontacts. "Type" fields categorize names for sorting as the user defines. "Other data" fields store information such as purchase and credit history, telephone call records, or interests.

Has massive storage capabilities. Holds up to 255 lines of comments for each name, plus unlimited time and date stamped notes. Features perpetual calendar, and automatic telephone dialing. Built-in word processing and merge gives the ability to pull in the information already keyed into the fields into individual or form letters. Prints mail labels, rotary file cards, and phone directories. This program is a great contact manager — call 1-800-228-2275 for information. *Requires a hard disk, 640K RAM and 80 column display. (Autodial feature requires modem.)*

International Business

Export Now

Book

Prepares a business to enter the export market. Clearly explains the basics, then articulates specific requirements for export licensing, preparation of documents, payment methods, packaging, and shipping. Includes advice on evaluating foreign representatives, planning international marketing strategies, and discovering official U.S. policy for various countries and regions. Lists sources.

EXECARDS®
International Communication Cards

EXECARDS offer unique cards you can send to businesspeople of many nationalities to help build and maintain lasting relationships. One distinguished EXECARD choice is a richly textured and embossed white card of substantial quality that expresses thank you in thirteen languages; Japanese, Russian, French, Chinese, Arabic, German, Swahili, Italian, Polish, Spanish, Hebrew, and Swedish, as well as English. Another handsome option is an ivory card with thank you embossed in Russian and English. To

Now – Find Out How Your Business Can Profit By Being Environmentally Aware

The Business Environmental Handbook

Book

Save your business while you are saving the planet. Here's your chance to learn about the hundreds of ways any business can help secure its future by starting to conserve resources now. This book reveals little-understood but simple techniques for recycling, precycling, and conservation that can save your business money now, and help preserve resources. Also gives tips on "green marketing" to customers .

Give yourself and your business every chance to succeed. Order the business tools you need today. Call 800-228-2275.

Gain the power of increased knowledge — Oasis is your source.

Acquiring Outside Capital

Raising Capital: How to Write a Financing Proposal

New Book

Valuable resource for writing and presenting a winning loan proposal. Includes professional tips on how to write the proposal. Presents detailed examples of the four most common types of proposals to secure venture capital and loans: Private Placement Circular; Prospectus or Public Offering; Financing Proposal; and Limited Partnership Offering.

The Money Connection: Where & How to Apply for Business Loans

Book

Comprehensive listing of funding sources. Lists hundreds of current nationally recognized business loan and venture capital firms. Describes the latest federal, state, county, and community loan, investment and assistance programs. Gives addresses and phone numbers of federal agency offices in each state.

Financing Your Small Business

Book

Essential techniques to successfully identify, approach, attract, and manage sources of financing. Shows how to gain the full benefits of debt financing while minimizing its risks. Outlines all types of financing and walks you step by step through the process, from evaluating short-term credit options, through negotiating a long-term loan, to deciding whether to go public.

The Loan Package

Book

Preparatory package for a business loan proposal. Worksheets help analyze cash needs and articulate business focus. Includes sample forms for balance sheets, income statements, projections, and budget reports. Screening sheets rank potential lenders to shorten the time involved in getting the loan.

The Successful Business Plan: Secrets & Strategies

Book and software for IBM & compatibles

Now you can find out what venture capitalists and bankers really want to see before they will fund a company. This book gives you their personal tips and insights. The Abrams Method of Flow-Through Financials breaks down the chore into easy to manage steps, so you can end up with a fundable proposal. Software is available for this book—see the back page of this catalog or call 1-800-228-2275 for a free software catalog. *Software requires a hard drive.*

Financial Templates
Software for IBM & compatibles

Software speeds business calculations. Includes 28 financial templates including various projections, statements, ratios, histories, amortizations, and cash flows. This is just one of many useful software packages designed specifically for small businesses. Call 1-800-228-2275 for information. *Requires Lotus 1-2-3, Microsoft Excel 2.0 or higher.*

Human Resource Ideas

A Company Policy and Personnel Workbook

Book and software for IBM & compatibles

Saves costly consultant or staff hours in creating company personnel policies. Provides model policies on topics such as employee safety, leave of absence, flextime, smoking, substance abuse, sexual harassment, performance improvement, grievance procedure. For each subject, practical and legal ramifications are explained, then a choice of alternate policies presented. Software is available for this book. Check our software catalog or call 1-800-228-2275 for more information.

People Investment

Book

Written for the business owner or manager who is not a personnel specialist. Explains what you must know to make your hiring decisions pay off for everyone. Learn more about the Americans With Disabilities Act (ADA), Medical and Family Leave, and more.

Managing People: A Practical Guide

Book

Focuses on developing the art of working with people to maximize the productivity and satisfaction of both manager and employees. Discussions, exercises, and self-tests boost skills in communicating, delegating, motivating, developing teams, goal-setting, adapting to change, and coping with stress.

Safety Law Compliance Manual for California Businesses

Book

Now every California employer must have an Injury and Illness Prevention Program that meets the specific requirements of Senate Bill 198. Already, thousands of citations have been issued to companies who did not comply with all seven components of the complicated new law. Avoid fines by using this guide to set up a program that will meet Cal/OSHA standards. Includes forms.

Plus optional binder for your company's safety program

Also available — Company Injury and Illness Prevention Program Binder — Pre-organized and ready-to-use with forms, tabs, logs and sample documents. Saves your company time, work, and worry.

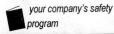
Why hesitate? If any product you order doesn't meet your needs, just return it for full refund or credit. 800-228-2275.

Unique cards get you noticed. Books & software save you time.

Business Communications

Proposal Development: How to Respond and Win the Bid

Book

Orchestrates a successful proposal from preliminary planning to clinching the deal. Shows by explanation and example how to: determine what to include; create text, illustrations, tables, exhibits, and appendices; how to format (using either traditional methods or desktop publishing); meet the special requirements of government proposals; set up and follow a schedule.

Write Your Own Business Contracts

Book

Explains the "do's"and "don'ts" of contract writing so any person in business can do the preparatory work in drafting contracts before hiring an attorney for final review. Gives a working knowledge of the various types of business agreements, plus tips on how to prepare for the unexpected.

Complete Book of Business Forms
Book

Over 200 reproducible forms for all types of business needs: personnel, employment, finance, production flow, operations, sales, marketing, order entry, and general administration. Time-saving, uniform, coordinated way to record and locate important business information.

EXECARDS®
The Original Business-To-Business Communication Tools

EXECARDS, business-to-business message cards, are an effective vehicle for maintaining personal contacts in this era of rushed, highly-technical communications. A card takes only seconds and a few cents to send, but can memorably tell customers, clients, prospects, or co-workers that their relationship is valued. Many styles and messages to choose from for thanking, acknowledging, inviting, reminding, prospecting, following up, etc. *Please call 800-228-2275 for complete catalog.*

PlanningTools™
Paper pads, 3-hole punched

Handsome PlanningTools help organize thoughts and record notes, actions, plans, and deadlines, so important information and responsibilities do not get lost or forgotten. Specific PlanningTools organize different needs, such as Calendar Notes, Progress/Activity Record, Project Plan/Record, Week's Priority Planner, Make-A-Month Calendar, and Milestone Chart. *Please call 800-228-2275 for information.*

Business Relocation

Company Relocation Handbook: Making the Right Move

Book

Comprehensive guide to moving a business. Begins with defining objectives for moving and evaluating whether relocating will actually solve more problems than it creates. Worksheets compare prospective locations, using rating scales for physical plant, equipment, personnel, and geographic considerations. Sets up a schedule for dealing with logistics.

Future Financial Planning

Secure Your Future: Financial Planning at Any Age

Book

Do-it-yourself workbook for setting up a retirement plan that can easily be maintained and followed. Covers establishing net worth, retirement goals, budgets, and a plan for asset acquisition, preservation, and growth. Discusses realistic expectations for Social Security, Medicare, and health care alternatives. Features special sections for business owners.

Mail Order

Mail Order Legal Guide

New Book

For companies that use the mail to market their products or services, as well as for mail order businesses, this book clarifies complex regulations so penalties can be avoided. Gives state-by-state legal requirements, plus information on Federal Trade Commission guidelines and rules covering delivery dates, advertising, sales taxes, unfair trade practices, and consumer protection.

Need it tomorrow? In most cases that's possible if you order before noon, PST. Just give us a call at 800-228-2275.

RR 3 9 4

BOOKS FROM THE OASIS PRESS® Please check the edition (binder or paperback) of your choice

TITLE	BINDER	PAPERBACK	QUANTITY	COST
The Business Environmental Handbook		☐ $ 19.95		
Business Owner's Guide to Accounting & Bookkeeping		☐ $ 19.95		
Buyer's Guide to Business Insurance	☐ $ 39.95	☐ $ 19.95		
California Corporation Formation Package and Minute Book	☐ $ 39.95	☐ $ 29.95		
Collection Techniques for a Small Business	☐ $ 39.95	☐ $ 19.95		
A Company Policy and Personnel Workbook	☐ $ 49.95	☐ $ 29.95		
Company Relocation Handbook	☐ $ 39.95	☐ $ 19.95		
Complete Book of Business Forms	☐ $ 49.95	☐ $ 19.95		
Controlling Your Company's Freight Costs	☐ $ 39.95			
The Essential Corporation Handbook		☐ $ 19.95		
Export Now	☐ $ 39.95	☐ $ 19.95		
Financial Management Techniques For Small Business	☐ $ 39.95	☐ $ 19.95		
Financing Your Small Business		☐ $ 19.95		
Franchise Bible	☐ $ 39.95	☐ $ 19.95		
Home Business Made Easy		☐ $ 19.95		
How to Develop & Market Creative Business Ideas		☐ $ 14.95		
Know Your Market: How to do Low-Cost Market Research	☐ $ 39.95	☐ $ 19.95		
The Loan Package	☐ $ 39.95			
Mail Order Legal Guide	☐ $ 45.00	☐ $ 29.95		
Managing People: A Practical Guide	☐ $ 39.95	☐ $ 19.95		
The Money Connection	☐ $ 39.95	☐ $ 24.95		
People Investment	☐ $ 39.95	☐ $ 19.95		
Power Marketing for Small Business	☐ $ 39.95	☐ $ 19.95		
Proposal Development: How to Respond and Win the Bid (hardback book)	☐ $ 39.95	☐ $ 19.95		
Raising Capital	☐ $ 39.95	☐ $ 19.95		
Safety Law Compliance Manual for California Businesses		☐ $ 24.95		
Company Illness & Injury Prevention Program Binder (OR Get kit WITH BOOK AND binder $49.95)	☐ $ 34.95	☐ $ 49.95 BOOK & BINDER KIT		
Secrets to Buying & Selling a Business	☐ $ 39.95	☐ $ 19.95		
Secure Your Future: Financial Planning at Any Age	☐ $ 39.95	☐ $ 19.95		
Start Your Business		☐ $ 8.95		
Starting and Operating A Business in... book INCLUDES FEDERAL section PLUS ONE STATE SECTION —	☐ $ 29.95	☐ $ 24.95		
PLEASE SPECIFY WHICH STATE(S) YOU WANT:				
STATE SECTION ONLY (BINDER NOT INCLUDED) – SPECIFY STATES:	☐ $ 8.95			
U.S. EDITION (FEDERAL SECTION – 50 STATES AND WASHINGTON, D.C. IN 11-BINDER SET)	☐ $295.00			
Successful Business Plan: Secrets & Strategies (GET THE BINDER...IT'S A BUSINESS PLAN KIT)	☐ $ 49.95	☐ $ 21.95		
Surviving and Prospering in a Business Partnership	☐ $ 39.95	☐ $ 19.95		
Top Tax Saving Ideas for Today's Small Business		☐ $ 14.95		
Write Your Own Business Contracts (HARDBACK BOOK)	☐ $ 39.95	☐ $ 19.95		

BOOK TOTAL (Please enter on other side also for grand total)

SOFTWARE Please check whether you use Macintosh or 3-1/2" Disk for IBM-PC & Compatibles

TITLE	3-1/2" IBM Disk	Mac	Price	QUANTITY	COST
California Corporation Formation Package Software	☐	☐	$ 39.95		
★ California Corporation Formation Binder book & Software	☐	☐	$ 69.95		
Company Policy & Personnel Software (Standalone)	☐		$ 99.95		
★ Company Policy & Personnel Binder book & Software (Standalone)	☐		$125.95		
Customer Information & Tracking System	☐		$119.95		
Financial Management Techniques	☐		$ 99.95		
★ Financial Management Techniques Binder book & Software	☐		$129.95		
Financial Templates	☐		$ 69.95		
The Small Business Expert	☐		$ 34.95		
Successful Business Plan (Full Standalone)	☐		$ 99.95		
★ Successful Business Plan Binder book & Software (Full Standalone)	☐		$125.95		

SOFTWARE TOTAL (Please enter on other side also for grand total)

Please add above totals on other side to complete your order. Thanks!

PSI Successful Business Library / Tools for Business Success Order Form (please see other side also)
Call, Mail or Fax to: PSI Research, 300 North Valley Drive, Grants Pass, OR 97526 USA
Order Phone USA (800) 228-2275   Inquiries and International Orders (503) 479-9464   FAX (503) 476-1479

Sold to: PLEASE GIVE STREET ADDRESS NOT P.O. BOX FOR SHIPPING

Name _____   Title: _____

Company _____   Daytime Telephone: _____

Street Address _____

City/State/Zip _____

☐ YES, I want to receive the PSI newsletter, ✳MEMO.
    Be sure to include: Name, address, and telephone number above.

Ship to: (if different) PLEASE GIVE STREET ADDRESS NOT P.O. BOX FOR SHIPPING

Name _____

Title _____

Company _____

Street Address _____

City/State/Zip _____

Daytime Telephone _____

Payment Information:

☐ Check enclosed payable to PSI Research (When you enclose a check, UPS ground shipping is free within the Continental U.S.A.)

Charge - ☐ VISA ☐ MASTERCARD ☐ AMEX ☐ DISCOVER   Card Number: _____ Expires _____

Signature: _____   Name on card: _____

EXECARDS — The Proven & Chosen Method of Personal Business Communications

ITEM	PRICE EACH	QUANTITY	COST
EXECARDS Thank You Assortment (12 assorted thank you cards)	$ 12.95		
EXECARDS Recognition Assortment (12 assorted appreciation cards)	$ 12.95		
EXECARDS Marketing Assortment (12 assorted marketing cards)	$ 12.95		
EXECARDS TOTAL (Please enter below also for grand total)			$

Many additional options available, including custom imprinting of your company's name, logo or message. Please request a complete catalog. 800-228-2275

PLANNING TOOLS — Action Tracking Note Pads — 8½" x 11"

ITEM		NUMBER OF PADS
Calendar Note Pad	☐ 1994	
	☐ 94/95	
	☐ 1995	
Total number of pads		
Multiply by unit price: x		
PLANNING TOOLS TOTAL	$	

UNIT PRICE FOR ANY COMBINATION OF PLANNING TOOLS
1-9 pads $3.95 each
10-49 pads $3.49 each
50 or more pads $2.98 each

SAFETY PROGRAM FORMS

ITEM	PRICE EACH	QUANTITY
Employee Warning Notification (Package of 20)	$4.95	
Request for Safety Orientation (Package of 20)	$4.95	
Report of Potential Hazard (Package of 20)	$4.95	
SAFETY PROGRAM FORMS TOTAL	$	

YOUR GRAND TOTAL

BOOK TOTAL (from other side)	$
SOFTWARE TOTAL (from other side)	$
EXECARDS TOTAL	$
PLANNING TOOLS TOTAL	$
SAFETY PROGRAM FORMS TOTAL	$
TOTAL ORDER	$

Rush service is available. Please call us for details.

Please send me:

_____ EXECARDS Catalog

_____ Oasis Press Software Information

_____ Oasis Press Book Information

Use this form to register for advance notification of updates, new books and software releases, plus special customer discounts!

Please answer these questions to let us know how our products are working for you, and what we could do to serve you better.

Title of book or software purchased from us: _____

It is a:
- ☐ Binder book
- ☐ Paperback book
- ☐ Book/software combination
- ☐ Software only

Rate this product's overall quality of information:
- ☐ Excellent
- ☐ Good
- ☐ Fair
- ☐ Poor

Rate the quality of printed materials:
- ☐ Excellent
- ☐ Good
- ☐ Fair
- ☐ Poor

Rate the format:
- ☐ Excellent
- ☐ Good
- ☐ Fair
- ☐ Poor

Did the product provide what you needed?
- ☐ Yes ☐ No

If not, what should be added? _____
_____
_____
_____
_____

This product is:
- ☐ Clear and easy to follow
- ☐ Too complicated
- ☐ Too elementary

Were the worksheets (if any) easy to use?
- ☐ Yes ☐ No ☐ N/A

Should we include:
- ☐ More worksheets
- ☐ Fewer worksheets
- ☐ No worksheets

How do you feel about the price?
- ☐ Lower than expected
- ☐ About right
- ☐ Too expensive

How many employees are in your company?
- ☐ Under 10 employees
- ☐ 10 – 50 employees
- ☐ 51 – 99 employees
- ☐ 100 – 250 employees
- ☐ Over 250 employees

How many people in the city your company is in?
- ☐ 50,000 – 100,000
- ☐ 100,000 – 500,000
- ☐ 500,000 – 1,000,000
- ☐ Over 1,000,000
- ☐ Rural (under 50,000)

What is your type of business?
- ☐ Retail
- ☐ Service
- ☐ Government
- ☐ Manufacturing
- ☐ Distributor
- ☐ Education

What types of products or services do you sell?
_____
_____
_____
_____

What is your position in the company?
(please check one)
- ☐ Owner
- ☐ Administration
- ☐ Sales/marketing
- ☐ Finance
- ☐ Human resources
- ☐ Production
- ☐ Operations
- ☐ Computer/MIS

How did you learn about this product?
- ☐ Recommended by a friend
- ☐ Used in a seminar or class
- ☐ Have used other PSI products
- ☐ Received a mailing
- ☐ Saw in bookstore
- ☐ Saw in library
- ☐ Saw review in:
  - ☐ Newspaper
  - ☐ Magazine
  - ☐ TV/Radio

Where did you buy this product?
- ☐ Catalog
- ☐ Bookstore
- ☐ Office supply
- ☐ Consultant
- ☐ Other_____

Would you purchase other business tools from us?
- ☐ Yes ☐ No

If so, which products interest you?
- ☐ EXECARDS® Communication Tools
- ☐ Books for business
- ☐ Software

Would you recommend this product to a friend?
- ☐ Yes ☐ No

If you'd like us to send associates or friends a catalog, just list names and addresses on back.

Do you use a personal computer for business?
- ☐ Yes ☐ No

If yes, which?
- ☐ IBM/compatible
- ☐ Macintosh

Check all the ways you use computers:
- ☐ Word processing
- ☐ Accounting
- ☐ Spreadsheet
- ☐ Inventory
- ☐ Order processing
- ☐ Design/graphics
- ☐ General data base
- ☐ Customer information
- ☐ Scheduling

May we call you to follow up on your comments?
- ☐ Yes ☐ No

May we add your name to our mailing list?
- ☐ Yes ☐ No

If there is anything you think we should do to improve this product, please describe: _____
_____
_____
_____

Thank you for your patience in answering the above questions.
Just fill in your name and address here, fold (see back) and mail.

Name _____
Title_____
Company _____
Phone _____
Address _____
City/State/Zip _____

If you have friends or associates who might appreciate receiving our catalogs, please list here. Thanks!

Name_____

Title_____

Company_____

Phone_____

Address_____

City/State/Zip_____

Name_____

Title_____

Company_____

Phone_____

Address_____

City/State/Zip_____

FOLD HERE FIRST

BUSINESS REPLY MAIL

FIRST CLASS MAIL PERMIT NO. 002 MERLIN, OREGON

POSTAGE WILL BE PAID BY ADDRESSEE

PSI Research
PO BOX 1414
Merlin OR 97532-9900

NO POSTAGE
NECESSARY
IF MAILED
IN THE
UNITED STATES

Please cut
along this
vertical line,
fold twice,
tape together
and mail.
Thanks!